THE STOCK EXCHANGE

THE
STOCK EXCHANGE

An Introduction for Investors

by

H. D. BERMAN, M.A. (Oxon.)

SIXTH EDITION

Edited by K. R. PINKER

PITMAN PUBLISHING

Sixth edition 1971
First Paperback edition 1971
Revised and Reprinted 1973

SIR ISAAC PITMAN AND SONS LTD
Pitman House, Parker Street, Kingsway, London, WC2B 5PB
P.O. Box 46038, Portal Street, Nairobi, Kenya

SIR ISAAC PITMAN (AUST.) PTY LTD
Pitman House, 158 Bouverie Street, Carlton, Victoria 3053, Australia

PITMAN PUBLISHING COMPANY S.A. LTD
P.O. Box 11231, Johannesburg, South Africa

PITMAN PUBLISHING CORPORATION
6 East 43rd Street, New York, N.Y. 10017, U.S.A.

SIR ISAAC PITMAN (CANADA) LTD
495 Wellington Street West, Toronto 135, Canada

THE COPP CLARK PUBLISHING COMPANY
517 Wellington Street West, Toronto 135, Canada

Cased edition ISBN: 0 273 31582 x
Paperback edition ISBN: 0 273 31585 4

Printed in Great Britain by
WESTERN PRINTING SERVICES LTD., BRISTOL
(B862/1025:43)

Foreword to the Fourth Edition

By the Rt. Hon. The Lord Ritchie of Dundee
Chairman, of the Stock Exchange, London

I AM pleased to have been asked to write a foreword to the fourth edition of Mr. Berman's interesting and informative book. The new edition appears at a time when the demand for knowledge about the Stock Exchange is constantly increasing.

The Survey on Savings and Attitudes to Shareowning, carried out by the Wider Share Ownership Council in February 1962, concluded that about three and a half million people in this country are direct investors in stocks and shares today. It also concluded that the same number of people—though not investors—had more than £500 in long-term savings and might be regarded as potential shareowners, and particularly that among non-investors younger people showed a greater interest in investment on the Stock Exchange.

All this means that more and more people will need responsible advice on Stock Exchange procedure and investment.

Mr. Berman has for many years been one of the leading members of the Stock Exchange panel of lecturers. He has lectured on Stock Exchange Law and Practice at the City of London College and has been an examiner on Stock Exchange subjects for the Royal Society of Arts.

This new and fourth edition of his book will be most useful in assisting both the new and the more sophisticated investor. It describes, from the insider's point of view, how the Stock Exchange works, and explains in a straightforward and comprehensible form its jargon and complicated procedure. It also offers in general terms some sensible and useful investment advice, based on Mr. Berman's own thirty years' experience as a Member of the Stock Exchange.

October, 1962   RITCHIE OF DUNDEE

Preface to the Sixth Edition

THE constant function of the Stock Exchange is to provide a market in which securities may be bought and sold and to facilitate the raising of money by Governments, Municipalities and public companies.

A book which describes this function can, however, never be completely up to date because, although the basic facts remain the same, important details are continually being changed, sometimes by the Government and sometimes by the Council of the Stock Exchange.

The previous edition explained the new method of transferring registered securities from seller to buyer, resulting from the Stock Transfer Act, 1963; both the old and the new methods are explained in the present edition because the latter is used for all United Kingdom securities while the old method remains in use for most Australian, some South African and for certain other securities.

The fifth edition also dealt with Capital Gains Tax and Corporation Tax and the results to be expected therefrom.

Protests produced some modification of the Capital Gains Tax on gilt-edged stocks but the prices of British Government loans continued to fall and the Finance Act of 1969 exempted gains on British Government securities from liability to capital gains tax provided they had been held for over a year. It is thought that this concession was made in order to attract buyers of British Government loans and thus improve the credit standing of the Government; it cannot have been made from any sense of justice as it deprived those who had bought Consols, War Loan or similar Government stocks from setting off their heavy losses against other gains. An investor who bought a redeemable debenture stock long ago on the strength of the redemption yield is virtually in the same position as a man who is fined now for committing an act which was perfectly legal at the time it was done but which is contrary to a law put on the Statute Book at a later date.

It had long been considered that the old system of taxation was too complicated but that it was reasonably fair in that it avoided taxing the same income more than once; it is interesting to note that France and Germany are believed to be considering the introduction of systems of taxation similar to that which this country has discarded.

The important point to mention here is that, as long as taxation remains at a high level, many of the best brains in the country will spend time on devising legal means of minimizing the tax liability to themselves, to their businesses or to their clients, when their energies could be employed more profitably from the national point of view in stimulating productivity and exports.

One can only hope that future changes in taxation will make the system simpler and more easily understood.

The recent changes in detail come under three headings—

STAMP DUTY. The rate of transfer stamp duty, which was changed in 1963, was again changed by the Finance Act, 1970; this also changed the rate of contract stamp duty. The latest rates are shown in the Appendix.

COMMISSIONS. The commission on gilt-edged stocks used to be charged on the nominal amount of the stock but is now charged on the consideration.

Apart from the scale of commissions chargeable to Country Brokers, which is not included in this book, there was only one commission scale. Now there are two scales; one for the commission to be charged on business initiated directly by the client, and another when the commission is to be shared with an agent introducing the business. To be eligible to receive a share of the commission (banks receive one-quarter and other agents, e.g. solicitors or accountants, receive one-fifth) the agent must be placed on the Stock Exchange Register of Agents and must pay an annual fee to the Stock Exchange.

These two scales of commission are printed in the Appendix.

DECIMALIZATION. The Stock Exchange may be said to have anticipated decimalization because $\frac{1}{64}$th of a pound ($3\frac{3}{4}$d. in the old currency), the smallest fraction normally used in the gilt-edged market, and $\frac{3}{4}$d. (old currency), the smallest amount normally used in quoting all except very low-priced shares, can be expressed as non-recurring decimals of a pound, whereas an old penny, halfpenny and farthing can only be expressed as recurring decimals.

Following the introduction of decimal currency on 15th February, 1971, the Stock Exchange Official List now prints quotations, marks and units of quotation in decimal form but jobbers in the gilt-edged market continue to quote prices in fractions down to $\frac{1}{64}$th and expressions such as "one-sixteenth to an eighth and over" continue to have their former meaning.

Jobbers in other markets quote prices in new pence and fractions, but fractions smaller than $\frac{1}{4}$ of a new penny are rarely used: expressions such as "close to close" seem to have disappeared.

Prices are quoted in new pence up to 999p; above that, they are quoted in pounds and fractions of a pound.

Prices in this book have been converted to decimals, although how the Stock Exchange will gradually adapt itself to the new conditions is still uncertain. The Stock Exchange computer has been programmed to accept fractions as small as one-sixteenth of a (new) penny (£0·000625) but was, temporarily, taken out of use because the work proved to be even more complicated than was realized.

This book was originally written for the inexperienced investor and care was taken to omit technicalities which did not concern him, while explaining those with which he was likely to be involved. Because the book is being increasingly used by students in preparation for their examinations, nine short chapters, commencing with Chapter XVIII "The Stock Exchange", which deal with technical points of Stock Exchange practice, have been added in this edition. Remarks on taxation have as we have said, been reduced to a minimum; this is such a complicated subject that it is best left to experts in the field.

This edition has been edited by Mr. K. R. Pinker to whom my thanks are due for much hard and efficient work.

H.D.B.

Contents

ix

CONTENTS

CHAPTER I

Introductory

THIS book was written, in the first instance, for the benefit of the inexperienced investor of every age and class. Its aim is, as far as possible, to answer the questions that he does not wish to ask for fear of showing his ignorance, and to show him how he can best co-operate with his stockbroker by saving both of them time and trouble by avoiding, in particular, the kind of misunderstanding which so often crops up and leads to expensive mistakes.

It is hardly necessary to point out that, if stockbrokers possessed the knowledge with which they are popularly credited, they would all have made their fortunes and retired long ago. It cannot be denied that some of them are wealthy, but the average stockbroker has to work hard in order to make a reasonable living just like any other business or professional man.

Just like any other business or professional man, he has developed his own jargon, which is merely a time-saving device, and one of the objects of this book is to explain this so that the reader can more easily understand his broker's letters.

I have, as far as possible, stuck to facts but, obviously, it is impossible to write a book of this nature without expressing opinions; some have been culled from letters to the papers or addresses to shareholders, and some are my own.

Since it is convenient in various examples to use shares in fictitious companies I have invented names and if, by some mischance, I have invented the name of a company which really exists, it is purely accidental.

This is not intended to be a comprehensive book and, while trying not to over-simplify, I have been careful to leave out matter that is of no particular interest to the ordinary investor.

The Stock Exchange is a market and, although many more people are now familiar with it than formerly, it still remains something of a mystery to the bulk of the population for two main reasons.

Unlike Covent Garden, Billingsgate, etc., where the producers attend to sell and the consumers to buy, the Stock Exchange is a two-way market in which the investors' and speculators' agents, i.e. the stockbrokers, are just as likely to be sellers as buyers; and, unlike Covent Garden, etc., the wares which are dealt in are "abstract."

When you buy a season ticket you pay your money, not for the piece of pasteboard which you receive, but for the right to travel to and fro as often as you wish during a certain number of days or weeks between two stations; the season ticket which, by the way, unlike stocks and shares, is non-transferable, is merely the evidence of your title to that right.

In the same way, stocks and shares confer the right to receive interest on part of a loan and the repayment of that particular part of the loan, if and when repayment is made, or to receive a share of the profits of a company; the piece of paper, the stock or share certificate which you receive, is merely the evidence of your title to that right and it is these abstract things, the rights to shares in capital and income, which are dealt in on the Stock Exchange, the bits of paper being merely incidental.

The Stock Exchange bridges the gap between governments, municipalities and companies which need to borrow money for long periods or to raise permanent capital, and investors who only wish to put up money for a comparatively short time.

The industrial revolution was bound up with the Stock Exchange and two important devices or inventions: the limited liability company, and the means of transferring securities from one owner to another.

The advent of the limited liability company made it possible for the first time for an investor to participate in the development of a project without thereby jeopardizing the whole of his personal fortune, and the means of transferring securities from one person to another made it possible for him to get his money back when he wanted it; it must be admitted that he cannot be sure of getting all, or even a part, of his money back, but against that drawback must be set the possibility of getting back more— sometimes even a great deal more—than he originally put in.

This possibility of getting back more than he put in is the

main inducement to put up capital, and profits must pay the capitalist for putting up the money instead of spending it—capital is defined by the economists as "postponed consumption" —and must pay him for taking the risk of losing part or all of his money.

The capital required nowadays is mostly very great; a man can still set up in business as a window cleaner with no more capital than is required to buy a ladder, a bucket and some chamois leather, but to set up a steelworks, an oil refinery or a cement plant needs millions.

In some industries an investment of £10,000 per man employed may be needed, and as more and more electronically controlled automatic equipment is used the amount invested per job created must rise much higher.

The Stock Exchange embodies much of the mechanism for raising money for great enterprises and for arranging for those who have put up the money to get it back when they want it by selling their holdings to fresh investors; if the facilities for getting their money back were lacking, they would probably never venture to put up the money in the first place and without that money, many well-known enterprises could never have come into being.

Some people regard the Stock Exchange as nothing more than a casino, but that is an entirely distorted view, though no one will deny that the facilities it provides are used for speculation. If a man stops to think he will be surprised to realize how many things he does are, in some measure, a speculation. If he is offered a good job and takes it he will quite possibly be offered a better one a few days later; if he rejects it, he may have to wait months before anything else nearly as good turns up. A similar situation might exist with a house or a second-hand car.

When buying or selling stocks and shares you can get plenty of more or less reliable information to help you to make a decision, although, as in all activities, there are unforeseeable factors which may make nonsense of your calculations, at any rate, from the short-term point of view.

It is not even easy to say where speculation begins because during the post-war years, inflation has undermined the status of gilt-edged securities, which used to be, and may one day again be, regarded as being "as safe as houses."

It may not be out of place to remark here that, while speculation carried to excess is undoubtedly an evil, reasonable
speculation, that is to say speculation within the means of the
individual concerned, serves a useful purpose in providing a
flow of business which makes it possible for the genuine investor
to buy more cheaply and to sell at better prices than would
otherwise be the case.

Speculation is apt also to have a steadying influence on
prices, since the speculator is always ready to sell a "bear" on a
sudden rise, thus having a sobering effect on the market, and to
support it on a sudden fall by buying back the shares of which he
is short, or opening new commitments on the "bull" tack when
he considers the fall has gone too far.

Although the Stock Exchange has often been attacked, it is
interesting that the Royal Commission, appointed in 1877 to
inquire into its constitution and customs, reported in the following year that the existence of the Stock Exchange and the coercive
action of its rules had been salutary to the interests of the public
and that the Stock Exchange Committee had acted uprightly,
honestly, and with a desire to do justice. Their conclusion, that
the Stock Exchange rules were "capable of affording relief and
exercising restraint far more prompt and often more satisfactory
than any within reach of the Courts of Law," accords well with
the report of the Cohen Commission on Company Law which
led up to the Companies Acts of 1947 and 1948. The Cohen
Commission commended the Stock Exchange on its reforms and
mentioned that Stock Exchange regulations could safely be
made more stringent than the law because, since they lacked
statutory authority, they could be waived or relaxed when the
merits of individual cases warranted it.

Since then the Council of the Stock Exchange have tightened
up the regulations to ensure that all possible relevant information should be given to intending investors before a Stock
Exchange quotation is granted; and the company concerned
has to undertake to notify a shareholder as soon as a transfer
out of his name is certified or presented for registration, and to
notify the Stock Exchange immediately of dividends and any
information necessary to enable the position of the company to
be appraised, so that the information may be disseminated at
once and the establishment of a false market avoided.

As a further measure to protect the public and to preserve the good name of the Stock Exchange, a Compensation Fund was instituted as long ago as 1950.

The Council of the Stock Exchange may, at their discretion, make payments out of this fund to a member of the public for any loss suffered through no fault of his own as a consequence of entrusting Stock Exchange business to a member of the Stock Exchange who has defaulted.

During the nineteen years to March, 1969, a total of £1,120,336 had been paid out as compensation and of this the Fund was only able to recover £345,031. In October, 1969, the London Fund stood at £710,408.

CHAPTER II

The Stock Exchange and Capital Structure

GOVERNMENT LOANS

If you want to invest money, the safest way is to lend it to the British Government direct—by depositing it with the National Savings Bank. As the Government cannot arrange profitably to borrow £500 from you today, £43 from Jones next week, and so on, and provide for repayment at short notice, it only pays $3\frac{1}{2}$ per cent per annum for money lent to it in this way—a rate of interest which is not very attractive, and the amount you may deposit is limited.

When the Government needed large sums of money, it issued loans for public subscription at rates of interest high enough to attract the money required; therefore, when you wish to invest money, you need not go to the Government and offer to lend it at the rate of $3\frac{1}{2}$ per cent (i.e. deposit the money in the Post Office Savings Bank) but you can arrange to take over a part of one of the Government loans and thus earn a higher rate of interest. In this case your broker buys as much of the loan as you require from someone who had lent money to the Government when the loan was issued.

The Government debt is not increased in this way; the Government merely owes the money to you instead of to Mr. Brown or Mr. Jones, and has to pay the interest on it to you, instead of to them.

The chief difference is that in the first case you lend, say, £100 to the Government on the understanding that interest at a certain rate ($3\frac{1}{2}$ per cent) will be paid to you and that the £100 will be returned to you at your request at any time on due notice being given. In the second case, you buy £100 of the loan at the market price, i.e. at a price low enough for you to be willing to pay it and high enough for the seller to be willing to accept it. This price depends on factors which will be discussed later.

6

If you buy £100 of a 4 per cent British Government loan you can be just as certain of receiving your £4 per annum interest on it as your are of receiving the £3·50 per annum on the £100 deposited in the Post Office Savings Bank, but you cannot be sure of receiving the £100 at any time; you cannot demand repayment from the Government and, if you wish to have the cash, you must sell your £100 of the 4 per cent loan at the market price of the day—this may be above or below the price which you originally paid. In fact, if you buy part of a Government loan, you have the chance of making a profit on it and run an equal risk of making a loss.

LIMITED LIABILITY COMPANIES

Formerly, when a man wished to undertake an enterprise which was too big for him by himself, he looked for one or more partners to help him not only with their work but also with their resources. This was not an entirely satisfactory arrangement because each partner or member of the company was liable, with the whole of his estate, for the debts of the company. Since, for enterprises such as building railways or large ships, starting a mine, etc., it was evidently necessary to have a large number of participants in the company in order to get sufficient capital and as few people would subscribe capital, knowing that by so doing they became liable for all the debts of the company, the Limited Liability Company came into being. In such a company, each member's liability is limited to the amount of capital which he agrees to subscribe; when he has paid this, he has no further liability. For example, suppose a man subscribes for 100 shares of £1 each at par: if the company calls up the whole amount at once, he pays £100 and has no further liability; if the company calls up £0·25 per share, he pays £25 and remains liable for £75. If he sells his £1 shares (£0·25 paid) the buyer is liable for £0·75 per share; if a call is made and the buyer is unable to meet it, the previous holder is liable if the call is made within one year of the time when the shares were transferred out of his name.

The Stock Exchange is the market which deals in Government loans and also in municipal loans, loans to foreign governments, loans to companies (debentures) and in the capital of companies.

The Stock Exchange being a private undertaking, only members and their clerks are admitted; for this reason, and also because the purchase and sale of securities of this kind is a complicated business, members of the general public are obliged to employ a broker to transact their business for them.

To justify the statement that this is a complicated business it may be pointed out that, if a man takes a stall in the market and fills it with potatoes it is assumed that he is there to sell potatoes and when the housewife appears with an empty market basket on her arm and stops in front of the stall there is little doubt that she is there to buy potatoes, provided only that they be cheap enough. Having bought her potatoes she proceeds to pay for them and take them away; there is no Government tax to pay— and the transaction is completed without the need for any documents.

In the Stock Exchange, however, a man is just as likely to be there to sell stock as to buy it; furthermore, the sums of money which the stock represents are often large and in the majority of cases the securities are not things which can be delivered from seller to buyer, like a sack of potatoes or even like a bank-note, but have to be transferred from the seller to the buyer by means of a legal document signed by the seller and, in some instances, also by the buyer and bearing, in many cases, an Inland Revenue Stamp of a value depending on the value of the security to be transferred.

CAPITAL OF A COMPANY

Apart from debenture or loan capital, a company's capital consists of stock or shares. Debenture and loan stocks, investment-trust preference stocks, some investment-trust ordinary stocks and one or two others, are quoted at so much per £100 stock (i.e. at so much per cent); most other stocks are quoted in units of any amount, the commonest being £1, 50p, 25p, 10p and 5p.

British Government stocks are transferable in multiples of one new penny, other stocks usually in multiples of a pound, with a minimum of £1; stocks quoted in units are transferable in multiples of the unit in which they are quoted. (There are one or two unimportant exceptions.)

Up to 1947 all shares had to have distinctive numbers, a requirement which entailed an enormous amount of work in the preparation of deeds of transfer and share certificates; in order to obviate this unnecessary labour many companies converted their fully paid shares into stock which is not numbered, transferable in units corresponding to the face value of the shares. This practice has one disadvantage when the units are not of £1: a client who has bought 400 stock units of £0·25 each may easily see the "£100 stock" on the certificate when it is sent to him, but overlook the "represented by 400 units of £0·25" immediately underneath, and ask where the other 300 are or, years later, intending to sell his whole holding, may tell his broker to sell 100 and then be surprised and, if the price has fallen meanwhile, pained, to find that he still has 300 units left when the balance certificate is sent to him.

The Companies Act, 1947, made it unnecessary for shares to have distinctive numbers provided that all the shares in that particular class were fully paid up and ranked *pari passu* for all purposes; and since 1947, there has been a tendency for unnumbered shares to replace units of stock. The word "shares" is often used indiscriminately for shares and for units of stock as the difference is only technical.

Shares may be of any denomination (the denomination of a share is its face or par value) and may be fully or partly paid. Since, except occasionally as a matter of coincidence, the face value of an equity share bears no relation to its price or to its intrinsic value and is, therefore, misleading, it is a great pity that English law does not allow companies to issue shares of "no par value" (n.p.v.). Shares of no par value are common in Canada and in the United States but, although proposals to authorize companies registered in this country to issue such shares have been made in Parliament, they have not yet been approved.

The holder of stock or shares in a company is a part-proprietor of the company and dividends may only be paid to him out of profits earned by the company.

Stock and shares can be of various classes, the names of which are more or less self-explanatory. Thus preference shares rank for dividends before the ordinary shares—it would be more correct to say that preference shareholders rank before the ordinary shareholders, but the meaning is clear—but they do not get anything more than their fixed rate of dividend, no matter how well the company may do; the first preference shares rank before the second preference, and so on. A cumulative preference share is entitled to the arrears of dividend before the ordinary shares get anything, should the company return to prosperity after a lean period, but a non-cumulative preference share enjoys no such right.

A participating preference share, as its name implies, is entitled to a fixed dividend in priority to the ordinary shares and to a further participation, which may or may not be limited, after a certain amount has been paid on the ordinary shares.

The ordinary shares are usually entitled to all that remains (the equity) after paying interest on the debentures and dividends on the preference shares and are, therefore, often referred to as equity shares or equities. Sometimes, however, they are divided into preferred ordinary and deferred ordinary shares, the former corresponding to a further class of non-cumulative preference or participating preference shares, and the latter to the ordinary shares in other companies.

There is no standardized nomenclature for the different classes of stocks or shares, so it is as well to look up their rights before investing in them. (The Stock Exchange Official Year Book, which is to be found in most reference libraries, gives all the particulars under the name of the company.)

Debenture holders are not proprietors, but creditors, of the company and interest has to be paid to them before any dividends can be distributed.

There is a further class of deferred shares which might more properly be described as "dividend deferred shares" or "temporarily deferred shares." One example is provided by Ampol Petroleum; the company wished to raise money to finance developments which would bring in no revenue for three or four years; this was done by making a rights issue of "dividend deferred shares" which received no dividend but which, at the end of three years, were automatically converted into ordinary shares.

A similar issue was made by Sovereign Securities, but in this case roughly one third of each holding of the "dividend deferred shares" was automatically converted into ordinary shares as soon as a dividend at a predetermined higher rate had been paid on the ordinary shares, and the balance was similarly converted when a higher dividend still had been paid.

CHAPTER III

Markets

THE price of a share, like the price of anything else, depends on the supply and the demand. Both supply and demand depend on a large number of factors, such as the past history of the company, the rate of dividend paid, the proportion of earnings usually distributed as dividend, the prospects of the industry in which the company is engaged, in general, and the prospects of the company in particular. Other factors are hopes or fears of a tariff, news of famine or revolution in one or other of the countries where the company's products are consumed, or which supply its raw materials; or, if the company is a railway, reports of good or bad crops in the agricultural districts, and estimates of the state of trade in the industrial centres which it serves. The marketability of the share is also a factor which affects the price.

The latter is a subject which appears to be understood by only a very small proportion of the general public, so that it may be as well to go into the matter fairly fully.

BROKERS AND JOBBERS

Members of the Stock Exchange, London, are divided into brokers and jobbers; brokers act as agents for their clients and buy and sell securities on their behalf. Jobbers are not allowed to deal with the general public but only with brokers or other jobbers; they specialize in certain securities, e.g. British Government stocks, oil companies' shares, brewery shares, etc. They "make" prices in the technical sense that, when a broker asks a jobber the price of a share, he replies, "I'll make you £1·20 to £1·22½" (or whatever the price may be); that means that he will buy shares at £1·20 or sell them at £1·22½.

The broker usually has in mind what he considers a fair

price; in this particular case he may consider that a 2p price is a fair price in Black Country Potteries in the prevailing market conditions. He checks his price with another jobber who also makes £1·20 to £1·22½ and with a third who makes him £1·20½ to £1·23. If he is a seller of 500 shares he says, "Sell you 500 at £1·20½" and the jobber confirms the deal by saying, "Buy 500 Black Countries at £1·20½" and the deal is done. If the broker were a buyer he would go back to the first jobber and buy 500 at £1·22½. If the market were rather more active he might try to find a 1p price between jobbers.

The point to be emphasized is that, when the jobber "makes" the price, he does not know whether the broker is a buyer or a seller. If he makes a wide price—makes a big difference between the price at which he is prepared to buy and the price at which he is prepared to sell—the broker will either demand a closer price before he deals or take the business elsewhere; if the jobber "reads" (guesses) the broker a buyer, and pitches the price rather high, he may find himself landed with shares at a higher price than he wished to pay if he has guessed wrong, or he may lose the business if he has guessed right. Once he has "made" a price he is bound to deal in the number of shares in which he has made it, or in a reasonable amount if no number has been specified, should the broker wish him to do so.

It must be pointed out that the jobber "makes" the price of a share only in a technical sense and that the popular idea that the Stock Exchange and its members raise and lower prices according to their whims is a fallacy. It is the investing public, including the big financial institutions, banks, insurance companies and investment trusts, as well as the large and small private investors, who determine prices in the long run. The jobber's aim is to make a living by buying securities and selling them at a profit or by selling securities and replacing them at a profit. If a particular jobber raises his price unduly, sellers will flock to do business with him and he will soon acquire a large number of shares which he cannot sell except at a loss; similarly, if he lowers his price too much, he will sell shares which he cannot replace without loss.

Jobbers are, therefore, forced to adjust their prices in accordance with the flow of buying and selling orders from the investing public, tempered with intelligent anticipation.

Thus, a tip in the daily Press that a certain share looks cheap will cause the jobbers to raise the price in anticipation of a stream of buying orders from the readers of the paper in question; they will only raise the price cautiously, however, since the tip may be regarded by existing shareholders as a welcome opportunity to get out with a small profit or, at any rate, without a loss after buying the shares for a quick profit and waiting for months without a sign of a rise.

There are three main reasons for buying stocks and shares: one is for investment, that is to say for the income which they will produce; one is for capital appreciation in the light of some expected development; and the third is a combination of the two.

There are two reasons for selling stocks and shares and the first really covers the second: the chief reason for selling is to raise money, whether it be to buy a house or a car or a business, or to pay death duties, or to buy other securities which at the moment appear more attractive, or to have money in the bank in the expectation of favourable opportunities of investing it to better advantage later on; the second reason is the belief that the particular stock or share to be sold is standing at a higher price than its real value, that is to say, a belief that the price is going to fall.

There is one other reason for buying and selling, and that is to take a profit or cut a loss on shares which have been sold or bought for a quick turn.

MARKETABILITY

Now for the question of marketability; if a company has a very large capital, the shares are likely to be widely held and there will always be shares "coming in" (to the market), from liquidation of deceased estates, from people taking profits on a slight rise in the price, from people cutting losses on a slight fall, or from other sources. In normal times there is an equally steady stream of buying orders and the shares are thus always changing hands. If a jobber is asked to make a price in a share of this kind (e.g. Courtaulds, which has over two hundred and sixty nine million £0·25 ordinary shares in issue, or the Imperial Tobacco Group Ltd., the ordinary capital of which consists of over five hundred and forty million £0·25 units of stock), he will make a fairly close price, knowing that, if the shares are sold to him, he will be able to dispose of them fairly easily while, if they are bought from him, he will have little difficulty in replacing them (in Stock Exchange jargon, he will have little trouble in getting his "book" even again). Further, a share of this kind is dealt in by a large number of jobbers, some of whom, on account of the state of their respective books, will make slightly different prices from the others. Take British Match, for example. At the time of writing the price is £2·70; one jobber may call them £2·67½–£2·72½ and refuse to "make" anything "inside" that. Presumably, his book is even and he does not wish to do business except at a wide price. Discreet inquiry might discover that another jobber calls them £2·70–£2·72½, while a third jobber calls them £2·69½–£2·72, so that the actual "touch" would be £2·70–£2·72; if the broker has an order to sell at £2·70, or at some lower price, he goes to the jobber who is making £2·70–£2·72½ and sells them to him at £2·70. If he has an order to buy at £2·72 or at some higher price, all that remains for him to do is to go and deal with the appropriate jobber, provided that the price has not moved against him during the time taken to make these inquiries. It should be noted that in active markets prices move very rapidly and a broker who has gone to the telephone to quote a price to a client may find that although there are telephone boxes inside the Stock Exchange the price has altered by the time he gets back into the market again.

The art of the good broker is to know when to deal and when to hold his hand and try for a better price; a jobber is not obliged to "make a price" and if a broker gets a name for squeezing the last farthing out of a deal when business is brisk, he may find himself unable to do business when conditions are difficult. Unless he is limited (i.e. has an order to execute at a price fixed by his client) a good broker will deal at a fair price without hesitation. He must be careful not to throw his client's money away, but it will react to the broker's disadvantage and through him to that of his clients in the long run, if he habitually tries to drive too hard a bargain.

Now, consider a company with a small capital of only one or two hundred thousand pounds. Being only a small company there are fewer people interested in it, and there are probably only two or three jobbers, and possibly only a single jobber, dealing in its shares; they will only make wide prices, knowing the difficulty they will have in getting their books even again if they deal, and will often refuse to make a price but ask the broker what he wants to do; if he tells them, they go and bid for or offer the shares to other brokers whom they know to be interested in the company, taking a "turn" out of the price to remunerate them for their trouble.

This is described as a "narrow" or difficult market, and the broker would probably have to tell his client that there was only a nominal price, dealing being a matter of negotiation on the basis of, for example, £1½ to £1⅞.

Marketability should also be taken into consideration when buying new issues; they usually come out with a flourish of trumpets and enjoy an active market for days, weeks or even months. After that, however, many of them fade away and gradually become more and more difficult to deal in.

In bad times the less well-known shares become difficult to buy and almost impossible to sell; the prices of the "blue chips" usually fall heavily as they can always be sold at a price. If money has to be raised, these are therefore the shares that are sold.

THE JOBBER'S TURN

The jobber's turn is usually regarded as the profit the jobber makes between buying and selling shares. Of course, if a jobber made 5¼ to 5⅝ in a share and went on alternately buying a hundred shares at 5¼ and selling a hundred shares at 5⅝ all day long he would make a very handsome profit. Unfortunately for him, however, it never happens just like that; usually when shares are sold to him in an active market other brokers have sold shares in the same company to other jobbers at the same price, and he may have to take a much smaller profit or either cut his loss or "nurse" the shares till the price improves again. Similarly, when he sells shares, he often finds that the price has risen when he tries to replace them. In the old days jobbers were always ready to put large lines of shares on their books and keep them till the market turned for the better, or else risk opening a big "bear" position until they could buy the shares back at a profit.

Jobbers still have to bear their losses in full but now have to surrender a large proportion of their profits to the tax collector; consequently their capital is diminishing and they can no longer afford to take the big risks that they could and did formerly. The result can be seen in the big price fluctuations caused by the purchase or sale of comparatively small amounts of stock or numbers of shares. Another factor making for big price fluctuations is that industrial company pension funds and insurance companies have bought large blocks of shares so that the floating supply of shares is much smaller than it used to be.

A broker has to bear in mind the sum of money involved in a bargain when deciding whether or not to deal. Thus, in dealing in 10,000 shares at £0·07½ (£750 cash consideration), he must remember that ¼p difference in the price represents about £25 whereas, when dealing in £750 stock at 100 (£750 cash consideration), a difference of $\frac{1}{32}$ in the price amounts to £0·23¾.

While writing about the jobber's turn it must be observed that the quotations shown in the papers (many newspapers now only give the middle price) and in the Official List are much wider than the prices actually made by the jobbers when it comes to dealing. If a broker cannot execute an order within the limits of the official quotation he is entitled to have the quotation altered. Most jobbers try to help their brokers and, particularly where out of the way shares in which there is no free market are concerned, it is not uncommon for a jobber to buy shares from a broker and then to come back and alter the bargain in the broker's favour on the grounds that he (the jobber) has sold the shares at a better price than he expected to get for them. It cannot be emphasized too often that it takes two to make a bargain; you cannot sell shares unless your broker can find someone willing to buy them from you, and you cannot buy shares unless he can find someone who is willing to sell. In the case of marketable securities buyers and sellers can always be found at a price but this is not so with shares which have only a restricted market.

A really free market depends to a great extent on differences of opinion. For instance, when a reduction in Bank Rate is announced Tom hurries to sell his insurance shares because he thinks that the insurance companies will have to invest the insurance premiums which keep on flowing in, on a lower yield basis. At the same time, Dick buys insurance shares on the grounds that the value of the companies' large holdings of gilt-edged stocks will appreciate in value.

MARKING BARGAINS

Bargains can be "marked" by either broker or jobber (or both) but only one mark at any particular price is recorded, and that not necessarily in the order in which the bargains have been done. The marks are recorded in the Official List, which is published every afternoon by the Stock Exchange authorities and copied in the *Financial Times* next day; bargains marked after 2.15 p.m. appear in the next day's list marked Φ indicating a bargain done on the previous business day.

Some brokers mark all their bargains, others only put in marks to protect themselves if they think they have dealt badly (either paid too much or accepted too little) as every broker is bound to do sooner or later.

A bargain marked ‡ indicates a special price; usually that either a jobber has bought a small number of shares or that an unusually large number of shares have changed hands.

The "marks" are sometimes misleading; a client wants to buy 1,000 shares in a rather obscure company at, say, £1·22½ and is incensed because his broker is unable to execute the order, although a bargain at £1·17½ was recorded on the previous day. It may well be discovered that a jobber who was a bear of two or three hundred shares managed to buy back fifty at £1·17½; until he can find a seller of several hundred shares he is not likely to agree to increase his bear position even at £1·22½.

DEALING

When one hears of a man offering so many thousands of pounds for a house it causes no comment, though it rings strangely in the ears of anybody connected with the Stock Exchange. There, a would-be buyer of shares always "bids" a price for them, while a would-be seller of shares "offers" them at a price; it is as well to follow this convention since it tends to prevent mistakes. The word "bid" informs the broker that the initiator of the business under discussion wishes to buy shares, while the word "offer" shows that the initiator of the business wishes to receive money in exchange for the shares that he has to sell.

The technique of dealing does not really concern the client very much but there is one point of Stock Exchange etiquette (which is little more than the principles of fair play analysed by common sense) of which he ought to be aware.

In order to be able to deal well a broker must be known, trusted and liked by the jobbers and to acquire their trust he must play fair.

When a jobber "makes" a price he is taking a risk and it is considered the proper thing for the broker to deal with the jobber who first made him the price that suited him. Thus, if a broker has an order to buy 100 shares at best and jobbers A, B and C "make" him £1·22½–£1·25, £1·23½–£1·26¼ and £1·22½–£1·25, respectively, he should go back to A and buy them from him if he is still making the same price; A will generally be "on" unless he has dealt with another broker meanwhile, in which case he may have altered his price. If A, B and C make £1·22½–£1·25, £1·23¾–£1·26¼ and £1·23–£1·25, respectively, the broker may deal with A on the grounds that he first offered him the shares at £1·25, or with C on the grounds that he made a closer price and, therefore, took a bigger risk; opinion among jobbers as to which is the correct course seems to be divided, however the Code of Dealing which was published for Members in 1968 opts for the latter course.

Suppose the price of a certain share is £0·76¼–£0·78¾ in the market; a jobber (A) approaches a broker and says, "I believe you have a client who might like to take £0·77½—go and bid him £0·77½ for 500." The broker rings you up and tells you; you are at liberty to say that you will not sell or that you want a higher price, but if you say that you will accept £0·77½ for 500 the deal is done at that moment (although the jobber does not know yet); your broker is not entitled to sell them at a higher price even if he hears jobber B openly bidding £0·78¾ while he is on his way to jobber A to tell him that the bid of £0·77½ has been accepted.

This may seem hard but it is only fair, since jobber A would still have to pay £0·77½ for the shares even if jobber B were offering them at £0·75 when the broker came back. Naturally, in a case of this kind, if the broker could not get you on the 'phone very quickly, he would go back to jobber A to report that the client was temporarily inaccessible and thus release him from his bid, and leave himself free to sell your shares at £0·78¾ supposing that he were looking after a limit for you at that price.

Another point is worth considering; you may see a share quoted at £1·31¼ in the paper, and write to your broker on Tuesday evening asking him to buy a certain number at about that price; on Thursday morning you get his contract for the purchase of the shares at £1·31¼ and naturally feel annoyed when you notice that the shares are quoted in the paper at £1·25; you feel that your broker has let you down. He probably felt discouraged at having taken a lot of trouble to buy them for you at £1·31¼, when he found them quoted at £1·30–£1·32½, only to see the price fall half an hour later; if only he had not been so conscientious but had gone out for a cup of coffee before executing your order, how much better he could have done for you! However, he cannot afford to gamble on the market moving the right way for you, and is bound to execute your order as quickly as possible as the price is just as likely to move the other way; if he waited and then had to pay considerably more, you would have a legitimate cause for complaint.

CHAPTER IV

Cash and Account Dealings

CLIENTS investing money for the first time often ask "When and how much do I have to pay? and what do I do with the contract?"

CONTRACTS

The contract note (this is often shortened to "the contract," an abbreviation which is used throughout this book) states that Black, Gray, White & Co., members of the Stock Exchange, have bought 100 Capstan & Winches Ltd. ordinary units at £1·01¼ by order and for account of John Smith, Esq., for the 6th May account, 19—; the consideration, commission, transfer expenses and contract stamp are set out separately, as well as the total. If Mr. Smith had bought Consols a similar contract note would have been sent to him, but "for the 6th May account, 19—" would have been replaced by "for cash" and there would have been no transfer expenses since no transfer stamp or registration fee is payable on British Government stocks.

The client should keep the contract, which is the only legal evidence he has to show that his brokers have bought the stock or shares for him at the price mentioned. It will also be needed for capital gains tax purposes. The total shown on the contract is the amount he has to pay; if the contract states "for cash" he should send his cheque to the broker at once; if "for the . . . (date) account," he should send his cheque to arrive not later than the morning of the date mentioned, if it is a town cheque, or a day or two (preferably three days) earlier if it is a country cheque.

DEALING FOR CASH

Bargains in British Government, Dominion and Colonial stocks, British Municipal stocks, and most new issues of stocks and shares, until they are fully paid and registered, are done for cash. Settlement takes place, theoretically, on the next business day after the day on which the bargain is done; in practice, it takes place within the next few days.

TRANSFER OF BRITISH GOVERNMENT SECURITIES

British Government securities are now almost entirely in the form of registered stock and registered bonds—certificates stating that the person or persons named therein[1] is/are the registered holder(s)—and a deed of transfer is required to transfer them from seller to buyer.

There may be a few bearer bonds left from before the 1939–45 War, but bearer bonds have again been issued during the last two or three years, probably because foreign investors are accustomed to bearer securities and therefore prefer them. Bearer bonds have been issued in respect of those British Government loans on which interest is payable free of tax to a resident abroad, with the exception of Treasury $6\frac{1}{2}$ per cent stock 1971 and Exchequer $6\frac{3}{4}$ per cent stock 1973; bearer bonds are also available for $2\frac{1}{2}$ per cent Consolidated stock, 4 per cent Consolidated, $3\frac{1}{2}$ per cent Conversion 1961 or after.

Bearer bonds are in the following denominations (often called "shapes")—

£50, £100, £200, £500, £1,000 and £5,000.

There may also still be a few holdings of the now obsolete inscribed stock for which no certificates have been issued; deeds of transfer in respect of inscribed stock have to be "certified" (*see* page 32, "Certification").

The books recording the names and addresses of holders of

[1] Incidentally, it may be of interest to note that the Bank of England will register U.K. Government securities in the names of the holder, for the time being, of some particular office, e.g. The Mess President, Wardroom Mess, H.M.S. . . . and when the stock is sold years later, the signature of another officer on the transfer, provided that he signs in his capacity of Mess President, is valid. Strangely enough the Bank is not empowered to register a Dominion stock in this way; it has to be registered in the name of the individual holding the office, and must be transferred by him to his successor.

British Government stocks are kept by the Bank of England; of the books of Dominion and Colonial stocks, some are kept by the Bank of England, others by the Bank of Montreal, the Commonwealth Bank of Australia, the Crown Agents for the Colonies, etc.

As no expense is incurred in the transfer of British Government securities and as, largely on account of this, bargains are often done in odd amounts, it is the practice to transfer stock from the seller to the immediate buyer, even if the latter has already sold part or all of it to a third person. Of course, if the buyer wants bearer bonds, he must buy multiples of the "shapes" available.

The selling broker (i.e. the broker of the client who has sold the stock) delivers the certificate and transfer signed by his client to the jobber who has bought the stock, against payment, and the jobber then lodges it with the Bank of England for registration. If the certificate is for a larger amount than that sold or if the transfer is in respect of inscribed stock for which no certificate has been issued, the transfer has to be certified before delivery.

When a client buys British Government stock the jobber from whom it was bought is entitled to deliver it on the next business day after the day of the bargain and as he is entitled to be paid on delivery the client should send his broker a cheque as soon as he receives the contract. Delivery is made by handing the buying broker a certified transfer (*see* page 32).

The broker fills in his client's full name and address on the transfer and lodges it with the Bank of England for registration. The stock certificate is ready in about a week or ten days and has to be collected and sent to the client or his bank to complete the transaction. When a client switches from one British Government stock to another, the broker often deals "stock against stock" which means that the jobber with whom he has dealt will not deliver and ask for payment until the broker delivers the stock sold by his client.

The Bank of England sends the interest on these stocks to the holder by post when it falls due but, like most company registrars, prefers to receive a dividend mandate with instructions to pay the interest to the bank at which the stockholder keeps his account.

DEALING FOR THE ACCOUNT

Other stocks and shares are dealt in "for the account." The arrangement of dealing for the account seems very simple to one inside the Stock Exchange, but it appears rather mysterious to those outside. Stock Exchange accounts last for a fortnight, except those accounts which cover Easter, Spring, Late Summer Bank Holiday and the Christmas and New Year holidays— these are extended to three weeks.

Formerly, dealing for the Account started on a Monday and continued until the following Friday week and this is still substantially the case; however, for technical reasons, any bargain made after 5.00 p.m. is deemed, for accounting purposes, to have been made on the following business day.

Any bargain made after 5 p.m. on the final day of the Account is dated the first day of the new Account, for settlement on the new Account Day. Bargains to close "bull" or "bear" positions may be done for "cash" on the Friday evening after 5 p.m., but closing bargains for cash may no longer be done on the morning of the first day of the new Account.

All bargains done during the fortnight between 5 p.m. on the

	FEBRUARY			MARCH			APRIL			MAY	
Dealing days for Settlement on—											
	28th Feb.			28th March			2nd May				
Sun.	.	.	.	.	.	.	.	.	.	.	.
Mon.	6	13	.	.	6	13	.	.	10	17	.	.
Tues.	7	14	.	(28)	7	14	.	(28)	11	18	.	(2)
Wed.	8	15	.	.	8	15	.	.	12	19	.	.
Thurs.	9	16*	.	.	9	16*	.	.	13	20*	.	.
Fri.	10	17*	.	.	10	17*	.	.	14	21*	.	.
Sat.	.	.	.	.	.	.	.	.	.	.	.	.

	14th March			18th April (3 weeks)			16th May		
Sun.	.	.	.	.	.	.	.	.	.	.	.
Mon.	.	.	20	27	.	.	20	27	‡	.	.	24	1	.	.
Tues.	.	.	21	28	.	(14)	.	21	28	4	.	(18)	.	25	2	.	(16)
Wed.	.	.	22	1	.	.	22	29	5	.	.	26	3	.	.
Thurs.	.	.	23	2*	.	.	23	30	6*	.	.	27	4*	.	.
Fri.	.	.	24	3*	.	.	24	†	7*	.	.	28	5*	.	.
Sat.	.	.	.	.	.	.	.	.	.	.	.	.

* Dealing for "new time" allowed.   † Good Friday.   ‡ Bank Holiday.

Friday and 5 p.m. on the Friday fortnight are due for settlement on the Account Day which is the Tuesday ten days after the day on which dealings ceased, the intervening time being taken up in preparing the transfer deeds, getting them signed, and so on. Dealing for future accounts is not allowed except that during the last two dealing days of each account "special" bargains may be made for the following account, and Options may be done, but not for a period beyond the seventh ensuing Account day.

Preparations for the settlement of each account take place while dealing for the following account is in progress.

The table on p. 23, in which alternate accounts are shown in the upper and lower parts, makes the overlapping clear; the dates shown are the days on which dealing takes place for settlement on the date shown in brackets in the same part of the table.

Specimen 1

BLACK, GRAY, WHITE & Co.   1,000 Throgmorton Street,

Partners   London, E.C.2.

A. B. Black   and Stock Exchange.

C. D. Gray

E. F. White

G. H. Robinson   24th April, 19....

Bought by order and for account of J. Smith Esq.

(Subject to the rules and regulations of the Stock Exchange).

		£
£1,600 2½% Consolidated Stock @ 29⅝		474·00
Contract stamp		0·10
Government transfer stamp		
Registration fee		
Commission ½% consideration		2·37
		£476·47

For settlement . . . Cash.

(Signed over 10p contract stamp)

BLACK, GRAY, WHITE & Co.

Members of the Stock Exchange, London.

Specimen 2

BLACK, GRAY, WHITE & Co.   1,000 Throgmorton Street,

Partners   London, E.C.2.

A. B. Black   and Stock Exchange.

C. D. Gray

E. F. White

G. H. Robinson   24th April, 19....

Bought by order and for account of John Smith Esq.

(Subject to the rules and regulations of the Stock Exchange.)

		£
450 Capstan and Winches Ltd. £1 units of ordinary stock @ £1·01¼		455·62
Contract stamp		0·10
Government transfer stamp		5·00
Registration fee		
Commission 1¼% money		5·69
		£466·41

For settlement 16th May, 19....

(Signed over 10p contract stamp)
BLACK, GRAY, WHITE & Co.
Members of the Stock Exchange, London.

Specimen 3

BARDOLPH AND COCKS

Partners
R. H. Cocks
T. Carter

201 Angel Court,
London, E.C.2.
and Stock Exchange.

Sold by order and for account of C. Brown, Esq.
(Subject to the rules and regulations of the Stock Exchange.)

		£
50 Canadian Pacific Railway ordinary shares @ £23·30		1165
Contract stamp	£0·30	
Commission ¾% consideration	£8·74	9·04
		£1155·96*

For settlement 24th August, 19....

(Signed over 30p contract stamp)
BARDOLPH AND COCKS
Members of the Stock Exchange, London.

* The above proceeds are subject to deduction in respect of the surrender of 25% of the dollar premium included in the price in accordance with Exchange Control regulations. With the dollar premium standing at 20% as it was at the time of writing, this would be worked out as follows:

£1155·96 (A) corresponds to 120% of value without premium

Value without premium = £1155·96 × $\frac{100}{120}$ = £963·33 (B)

Dollar premium = A–B = £192·63 of which one quarter = £48·16 has to be surrendered to Exchange Control. (See also, page 39.)

FOREIGN GOVERNMENT BONDS

Foreign Government loans, which are dealt in in London, are mostly in the form of bonds to bearer, the bonds being of various denominations from £10 to £1,000, those of £100 and £500 being the most common. Each bond has a sheet of coupons attached to it and both bonds and coupons are printed from plates engraved with intricate designs to prevent forgery. Each bond has a distinctive number and the coupons bear the number of the bond to which they are attached as well as the date on which they are due. These bonds and share warrants to bearer are known as "securities passing by delivery" since they are transferred from seller to buyer simply by handing them over just like a bank-note. The owner's name does not appear on the bond or warrant to bearer. In order to comply with the Exchange Control Act these bonds have to be deposited with an "authorized depositary," i.e. a bank, solicitor or stock-broker.

Owing to economic and political causes, including two world wars and revolutions ranging in importance from the Russian Revolution to comic-opera revolutions elsewhere, some of the foreign governments and foreign municipalities have defaulted on their obligations. Some, being more honest or more jealous of their financial good name than others, are meeting their obligations. Dealing in foreign bonds is now a very complicated business, the main complications coming under two heads.

First, a number of these loans were floated simultaneously in London, Paris, Berlin, Berne and New York with coupons payable in pounds, francs, marks or dollars at the holders' option at fixed rates of exchange; it is the dollar clause which is now the main one of practical importance and, though holders in this country are not allowed to encash their coupons in dollars, arrangements have been made for them to obtain the sterling equivalent at the current rate of exchange (i.e. about $2·40 = £1) of the dollars to which they would otherwise be entitled; this also applies to the bonds when redemption takes place.

This appears very involved but is quite intelligible if you remember that the £/$ exchange rate was $4·86⅔ = £1 when some of these loans were floated, $4·03 = £1 when some of the later loans appeared or new agreements were made, and is now $2\cdot40 = \pounds1$.

Two examples will make the matter clear—

1. *Japan* $5\frac{1}{2}$% *Conversion Loan issued in 1930.*

Coupons were payable in sterling in London or at $\$4\cdot86\frac{2}{3}$–$\pounds1$ in New York.

The coupon for six months' interest on a $\pounds100$ bond (nominally $\pounds2\cdot75$) on account of the dollar clause is now worth

$$\frac{\pounds2\cdot75 \times 4\cdot86\frac{2}{3}}{2\cdot40} = \pounds5\cdot57.$$

The $\pounds100$ bond, if the dollar/pound exchange rate is still $\$2\cdot40$–$\pounds1$ when it falls due for redemption, will be paid off at

$$\pounds100 \times \frac{4\cdot86\frac{2}{3}}{2\cdot40} = \pounds202\cdot78.$$

2. *German* $5\frac{1}{2}$% *Loan 1930 (Young Loan).*

Under the 1952 agreement Conversion Bonds (in denominations of $\pounds100$, $\pounds500$ and $\pounds1,000$) were issued in exchange for validated bonds of the original loan.

The adjusted nominal value of a $\pounds100$ Conversion Bond is $\pounds202\cdot78$ based on the original dollar clause at $\$4\cdot86\frac{2}{3}$ to $\pounds1$ and the $\pounds/\$$ rate on 1st August, 1952 Interest is payable at $4\frac{1}{2}$ per cent (instead of $5\frac{1}{2}$ per cent) on the adjusted nominal value, i.e. $4\frac{1}{2}$ per cent on $\pounds202\cdot78$ or $9\cdot12$ per cent on $\pounds100$.

Redemption by 1980 at latest is by sinking fund by purchase under or drawings at par ($\pounds202\cdot78$).

At 180 the flat yield is $5\cdot07$ per cent and the gross redemption yield is $5\cdot12$ per cent.

The second cause of complications is due to the arrangements made with their creditors by foreign governments and municipalities who defaulted on their obligations for one reason or another.

Japan always had a good name for meeting her obligations but, naturally, made no payments to British holders of her bonds while she was at war with this country. The post-war arrangement made with Japan is that on all bonds presented to be "enfaced" (rubber-stamped with a declaration that the beneficial owner had assented to the arrangement) interest due between 26th September, 1952, and 22nd December, 1952, was payable on 22nd December, 1952, interest payable thereafter was payable on the due dates, and interest due between 22nd December, 1942, and 26th September, 1952, became payable ten years after the date on which it was due.

In effect, from 1952 to 1962, inclusive, assented Japanese bonds paid double interest—current interest plus an equal amount of interest in arrears. The final redemption dates were extended for ten or fifteen years at the same rates of interest.

As no final date was fixed for assent to this scheme of arrangement, there are "Assented" and "Non-assented" bonds in the market; the latter have all coupons due since 1941 still attached (i.e. unpaid) and are particularly attractive to buyers not subject to United Kingdom income tax (e.g. residents abroad and charities not subject to tax) who can buy these bonds and, by "assenting," obtain payment of the gross amount of the coupons due to date.

Holders of non-assented bonds could sell them at about the price of the assented bonds plus the gross accrued interest, thus obtaining the interest in the form of capital; capital gains tax has put an end to that.

The various loans fall into different categories, depending on the political and economic conditions in the countries concerned and on their past records, the prices reflecting the market opinion of the chances of the obligations being met in full, partly or not at all.

Thus, the prices of Greek bonds vary from £15 to £40 per £100 bond, Chinese bonds from £0·50 to £2 per £100 bond, with bonds drawn for repayment—but not repaid—standing at lower prices than undrawn bonds, and Russian bonds at about £0·25 or £2 per £100 bond.

Incidentally, there is an amusing story, which is said to be true, to the effect that the price of one of the Russian Imperial Railway bonds rose from £0·37½ to about £0·75 per £100 on the discovery made by a certain stockbroker's wife that these bonds were printed on vellum which made very fine lampshades—however, not all Russian bonds are suitable for that purpose.

These prices suggest that nobody expects the U.S.S.R. ever to pay up on loans floated by Czarist Russia, that the possibility of trade with China gives some faint hope of an eventual resumption of reduced payments on Chinese Government loans, and that the chances of getting some payment out of Greece are slightly rosier.

Full particulars of foreign loans can be found in the Stock Exchange Official Intelligence which is kept in most public libraries; the object of this book is to point out some of the details for which you should look.

There is one other series of bonds which is of particular interest to surtax payers, being quite unlike other bonds, as the result of the latest scheme of arrangement with the creditors.

National Railways of Mexico bonds are now a direct obligation of the Mexican Government; under the 1946 scheme of arrangement entered into retrospectively some time after that date, holders were given the choice of two alternatives. Under Plan "A", which is no longer of any interest, the principal of each bond was scaled down to about one-fifth of its face value and interest at the contractual rate was payable on the reduced capital. These Plan "A" bonds have now been paid off. Under Plan "B" the bonds retained their face value but all interest payments ceased; the bonds are redeemable by purchase in the open market below the "drawing price," or, if the Mexican Government is unable to buy a sufficient number of bonds in any one year to comply with their obligations, bonds are drawn by lot each December for redemption in the following March at prices which rise each year until March, 1975, when the outstanding bonds have to be paid off at face value.

These bonds are United States dollar bonds, so that, with the exchange rate at $2·40 to £1, a $500 bond, if not drawn earlier for repayment at a lower price, would in 1975 be payable at

$$\$500 \div \$2 \cdot 40 = £208 \cdot 33$$

which compares very favourably with the prices of £115 per $500 bond of the 1951 series and £115 per $500 bond of the 1957 series.

Only about 1 per cent of these bonds will remain to be paid off in March, 1975, but, if your bonds are drawn earlier, although you will get a smaller profit, you will not have to wait so long for it.

TRANSFER OF REGISTERED STOCKS AND SHARES

The Stock Transfer Act, 1963, simplified the procedure but, as it did not apply to securities of all companies registered overseas, for example, in Kenya and South Africa, though many South African companies have now adopted it, the old method must still be described and, although the new procedure applies to the majority of Stock Exchange transactions, it is convenient to deal with the old method first.

A buyer of shares in South African companies must be charged with South African stamp duty amounting to one rand (£0·58) for every 100 rands, or part of 100 rands (£58·33) consideration. This rate was introduced by the 1968 South African Stamp Duty Act. Purchasers of shares on an Australian register are charged stamp duty of about 0·4 per cent on a sliding scale which varies on each of the three main Stock Exchanges.

The Stock Transfer Act, 1963, does not apply to shares which are to remain partly-paid more or less permanently; such shares are a rarity nowadays even if any still exist. However, it does apply to partly-paid new shares which are to become fully paid within a few weeks; these are in the form of allotment letters which do not have to be signed by the buyer before they are registered.

TRANSFER OF SECURITIES NOT SUBJECT TO STOCK TRANSFER ACT, 1963

On the Wednesday before account day the buying brokers (our old friends Black, Gray, White & Co.), that is to say, the brokers of the client who has bought the shares, make out a "ticket" stating the full name, description and address of their client, the number, name and price of the shares and the amount of the transfer stamp, and bearing the intimation that "Black, Gray, White & Co. pay." Their clerk goes to the settling room and puts the ticket in the "box" of the jobber from whom the shares were bought. The jobber may have bought and sold a large number of these shares during the account; if he has to deliver shares on balance he keeps the ticket, but, if not, he passes it on to a firm from whom he has bought shares. The ticket may thus pass through various hands before it reaches the ultimate sellers, Jones & Co., the brokers who sold the shares for Mr. Green.

The description in the case of a woman is "spinster," "married woman," "widow" or "feme sole"; in the case of a man it may be anything—baker, banker, civil servant, merchant, retired army officer, clerk or gentleman, but many companies consider the last too vague and refuse to accept it.

Jones & Co., having the share certificate, make out a deed of transfer (referred to as a "transfer" for short) filling in the seller's name, address and description exactly as on the certificate, and the buyer's name, etc., as on the ticket. If it is an old certificate the shareholder's address may be out of date, but that does not matter; if the new address is put in, "formerly of the old address" must be added so that the transfer will agree with the certificate. The consideration filled in on the transfer is the price on the ticket multiplied by the number of shares; this price is the price paid by the buyer and is often different from the price received by the seller, as there may have been intermediate transactions. If the shares have distinctive numbers the numbers of the shares to be transferred are copied on to the transfer from the share certificate.

Jones & Co. then send the transfer to Mr. Green to be signed and witnessed and returned to them; it should be remembered that the wife or husband of the signatory is usually not eligible as a witness. On receipt of the signed transfer, Jones & Co. have it stamped at the Inland Revenue Stamp Office and it is then ready for delivery. If Mr. Green lives in town, the transfer will probably be ready for delivery on account day but, if he lives in the country or abroad, there may be some delay in getting his signature.

If the transfer is for the same number of shares as the certificate, Jones & Co. deliver them together, with the ticket attached, to Black, Gray, White & Co. on the account day or as soon after as possible; Black, Gray, White & Co. pay for them on the day on which they receive them and Jones & Co. pay Mr. Green as well on the same day. Stock (i.e. stock, shares or bonds) must be delivered at the Central Delivery Department before 12.30 p.m. or to the buying broker's office by 1.15 p.m.; after that time the buyer need not accept them and the seller has to wait until the next day to deliver the stock and receive his money.

If Mr. Green has only sold part of his holding of shares, Jones & Co. take the transfer and certificate to the Stock Exchange Share and Loan Department or to the company's office for "certification." The Share and Loan Department, or the company, keep the certificate, issue a "balance receipt" which can be exchanged for a "balance certificate" (i.e. a certificate for the balance of the shares) in due course, and sign a declaration on the transfer certifying that a certificate for the number of shares mentioned therein has been deposited with them. Jones & Co. then deliver the certified transfer in the same way as described above.

Black, Gray, White & Co. forward the transfer to their client to be signed and witnessed and, on its return, send it to the company with the seller's certificate (unless it is a certified transfer) for registration; in due course (usually about two months) the company sends them (the brokers) a new certificate in their client's (the buyer's) name and they complete the transaction by forwarding the new certificate to their client or to his bank, according to his instructions. From time to time letters appear in the press asking why the address of the company does not appear on the certificate. Many certificates are kept for several years, during which time the company may change its address. Addresses of public companies appear in the Stock Exchange Official Year Book available in most public libraries.

Any alteration, deletion or erasure should be initialled by all the signatories or the transfer will not be accepted by the company.

The witnesses should give their full postal addresses so that the company can communicate with them in case of dispute; failure of the witness to give sufficient address may lead to the rejection of the transfer by the company, with consequent delay in the completion of the transaction. If the witness gives an address abroad the company will probably refuse to register the transfer until the signature has been attested by a British Consul or by a Notary Public.

When a client buys several hundred shares in a company, it is not uncommon for them to be delivered in small numbers from several different sellers and when they are sold again they may have to be delivered to several different buyers; as a matter of convenience many investors now arrange to have their shares registered in the name of a nominee (usually a company specially formed for the purpose by the investor's bank); one signature instructing the bank to take up so many shares from such and such a broker or to deliver so many shares to the broker is enough to complete the deal.

This arrangement is particularly valuable if the client has to go away from home, since it makes it unnecessary for transfers to be forwarded all round the country after him for his signature.

The bank then keeps the certificate in safe custody for its customer; incidentally, the bank is the safest place for all stock and share certificates, whether the shares are registered in the client's own name or in that of his bank.

When the shares are registered in the client's own name it is becoming increasingly common for him to send the company a dividend request form instructing the company to pay all dividends direct to his bank. This saves a certain amount of trouble and is a safeguard against loss in the post if the shareholder changes his address and forgets to notify the company.

A few companies charge a fee of $£0 \cdot 12\frac{1}{2}$ per document for registration. When a transfer is lodged with them they write to the transferor saying "we have received a transfer for . . . shares in the company out of your name into the name of . . . purporting to be signed by you; if we do not hear from you by return of post, we shall assume it to be in order," as a safeguard against fraud.

When a client buys stock his broker is entitled to be paid on the day on which the stock is delivered to him, since he must pay for it on the same day. As the stock may be delivered on account day or on any subsequent day, it is usual for the client to pay his broker on or before account day. If, however, the amount is large, it is often arranged that the broker should deliver the stock, as it comes in, to the client's bank against payment in proportion to the amount delivered; in this case the bank attends to the registration.

THE STOCK TRANSFER ACT, 1963

The Stock Transfer Act, 1963, applies to fully-paid-up registered securities of any description issued by a limited liability company or company incorporated by Royal Charter registered in the United Kingdom, securities issued by the Government of the United Kingdom (other than those on the Post Office register), securities issued by United Kingdom public boards and local authorities, and units of a unit trust scheme. The Stock Transfer Act over-rides articles of association specifying special forms of transfer deed.

The Act does not apply to securities issued by companies registered abroad, for example, in Australia, South Africa or Zambia, although such companies may be invited to adopt it provided that the law of the country of domicile does not preclude it.

The effect of the Act is, briefly, that the transferor (the seller) need sign only one form (the Stock Transfer), in respect of any number of shares or of any amount of stock sold at one time, and that his signature need not be witnessed; if the shares are registered in joint names, all the transferors must sign.

The Stock Transfer Form contains the name of the company and description of the security, the number of shares or the amount of stock sold and the full names of the transferors; if there is only one transferor, his full postal address is also given.

When the Stock Transfer is sent to the seller(s) for signature, it does not contain either the consideration or the name of the transferee (the buyer).

The buyer does not have to sign at all and it is for this reason that the Act applies only to fully-paid securities with no liability attaching to them. (Renunciation letters, whether nil-paid, partly-paid, or fully-paid, can now be registered in the buyer's name without his signature although they are not mentioned in the Act; nil-paid and partly-paid letters are bought in the full knowledge that payment in full will have to be made within a few months at the most and are very different from partly-paid shares, on which there is a liability which may never materialize.)

If all the shares sold are to be transferred to one buyer and the certificate is for the same number of shares, the seller's broker fills in the consideration on the Stock Transfer, has it stamped at the Stamp Office, and delivers it to the buyer's broker with the certificate attached. The buyer's broker fills in the name of the transferee (the buyer or his nominee) and sends the Stock Transfer and the certificate to the company for registration.

If the shares are to be delivered to several different buyers, the seller's broker makes out "Brokers Transfer Forms" which are exact copies of the Stock Transfer Form, except for the numbers of shares or amounts of stock; the Brokers Transfer Forms bear no signature.

The appropriate numbers of shares and considerations are filled in on each Brokers Transfer Form, and the Brokers Transfers are then stamped; when this has been done they are certified against the Stock Transfer Form and certificate, and a balance receipt for any shares covered by the certificate which have not been sold is obtained at the same time.

The certified Brokers Transfers are then delivered to the various buying brokers who complete and register them.

Some clients worry because they are accustomed to seeing the consideration stated on the transfer, but under the new system it no longer appears; incidentally, this puts an end to queries from (selling) clients who noticed that the consideration did not tally with the amount received by them but failed to see the footnote printed on the transfer form pointing out that by law the consideration shown must be that paid by the buyer, and that this would rarely be the same as that received by the seller.

The consideration is filled in either on the Stock Transfer after the seller has signed it, or on the Brokers Transfers, according to whether the shares are to be delivered to one or more separate buyers, as described above; the buyer never sees the transfer at all so it is more important than ever that he should make sure that his broker has his name, address, and registration instructions accurately noted.

Others are worried because the Stock Transfers sent to them by certain brokers are evidently carbon copies; but such documents are legal provided that they are clearly legible and that the ink is reasonably permanent. The reason for using carbon copies is that these brokers employ a special copying machine which is sensitive to black but insensitive to red ink; the Stock Transfers are prepared as carbon copies of a "master copy" on which the number of shares or amount of stock is typed in red and the rest in black ink. The master copy is kept in the office while the carbon copy is sent for signature. If there is more than one buyer, the requisite number of Brokers Transfers are made by running the master copy through the copying machine. As the number of shares is typed in red, to which the machine is insensitive, the Brokers Transfers prepared in this way have blank spaces which are then completed by filling in the appropriate numbers. This not only saves time but avoids typing mistakes in copying the original document.

The Stock Transfer Act has advantages over the old system, but there are disadvantages as well. The main advantages are that the seller need sign only one document in respect of any number of shares sold at one time and need not have his signature witnessed. As the Stock Transfer for any one sale can be prepared at once for a client with whom the broker regularly does business, or as soon as the broker receives the relative certificate in the case of a new client, the broker can usually get the Stock Transfer signed and returned to him well before account day so that delivery can be made promptly.

As there is no need to obtain the buyer's signature, the buying broker can register the securities without delay and thus reduce to a bare minimum, claims on the seller for dividends, and rights and capitalization issues. It is also hoped that the definitive certificates will be obtained much more quickly than formerly.

The disadvantages are that deliveries tend to be concentrated on the account day and the following day or two, so that the work in brokers' offices is much less evenly spread over the fortnightly account, although physical obstacles to prompt delivery are provided by queues for stamping and certification.

Another disadvantage is that, as the buyer never sees the transfer form, he is unable to detect errors in the spelling of his name and address; company registrars complain that they too suffer from headaches on that score.

It is thought that the new transfer system may make the perpetration of fraud less difficult than formerly, though there is reason to think that it will be much less easy than might appear at first sight.

CANADIAN AND AMERICAN SHARES

These shares are registered but the share certificates have a deed of transfer printed on the back; when this has been signed by the shareholder named on the face of the certificate (the space for the name of the person to whom the shares are to be transferred being left blank), the shares are delivered from seller to buyer in the same way as bearer shares (to be "good delivery" in London the certificates must in general be for ten—or a smaller number—shares each) except that the dividends are paid to the registered shareholder and must be claimed from him by the person who owns the shares (i.e. the person who has the share certificate in his legitimate possession).

Most of these shares stand in the names of finance houses, jobbers or brokers ("recognized marking names") who deal in them and who exchange the dollar dividends for sterling, deduct United Kingdom income tax and issue tax vouchers to the owners of the shares and charge a small commission for their services. The share certificates have to be presented to the registered shareholder to be "marked for dividend" before the dividend is paid; this is to prevent the same dividend being claimed twice over on the same shares. It is now usual for the registered holders to pay the dividends to the bank claiming them on the bank's undertaking to mark the certificates—this saves posting the certificates to and fro, and the bank issues the tax vouchers.

Unless otherwise instructed, a broker will deal for his client in shares in "recognized marking names" since shares in other names command a lower price and a less free market. If the buyer intends to hold the shares indefinitely and wishes to save the cost of collection of dividends, he can have them registered in his own name on payment of the registration expenses; if that is his intention, he should inform his broker when he gives him the buying order, as he may be able to save money by buying shares in "other" names; such a course is probably false economy and is not recommended.

When giving your broker an order to sell American or Canadian shares you should, at the same time, instruct your bank to send him the certificates; if you can tell your broker that the shares are in marking names, and not in your own name, that is all that is necessary.

Before the advent of decimalization, American and Canadian shares were dealt in in London in dollars; these, however, were neither American nor Canadian, but fictitious dollars worth 4s. each ($5 to £1). They were sometimes called "London dollars" and were also referred to as "dummy" dollars. This practice started long before the First World War, when dollars were worth approximately 4s. (the exchange rate never varied greatly from $4·86⅔–£1), to simplify the keeping of accounts, the difference between the standard rate of the fictitious dollar ($5–£1) and the actual rate of exchange on New York or Montreal being allowed for in quoting the price of the share. A price of $486⅔ in New York then would have been equivalent to a price of $500 London, both being equal to £100. The "dummy" dollar is no longer used and prices are now expressed in pounds, i.e. one fifth of the dummy dollar equivalent.

Exchange Control regulations restrict the purchase of dollar securities abroad except in so far as they are made with the proceeds of sales of dollar securities held in this country. The result is that the supply of investment dollars is limited and any stimulus to the demand for them—e.g. fears of a devaluation of the pound—raises the price, which is known as the dollar premium.

This premium is included in the price paid by buyers resident in the sterling area when buying dollar securities with pounds. It has risen as high as 60 per cent since the last devaluation of the pound.

The calculation is simple but involves some tedious arithmetic unless you have a slide rule or a "ready reckoner" made out for this purpose.

The formula is

$$\frac{\text{New York price}}{\text{exchange rate}} \times \frac{100 + \text{dollar premium}}{100}$$

e.g. if the exchange rate is $2·3925–£1 and the dollar premium 20 per cent, the London price is

$$\frac{\$140\frac{1}{2} \ (\text{N.Y. price})}{\$2·3925} \times \frac{100+20}{100} = £70·47$$

Since the New York and Montreal prices are "bid" prices, unless otherwise stated (i.e. the prices at which shares can be sold on the market), the London price must be raised slightly, since London prices are normally "middle prices", i.e. half-way between the prices at which shares can be sold and the prices at which they can be bought.

The law of this country requires all shares of companies registered in the United Kingdom to have a nominal value; the nominal or par value of an equity share is often misleading, since the whole of the equity shares is represented by all the assets of the company which are left after the debentures and preference shares have been provided for. A company may have one million ordinary shares; if the equity is worth £2 million, each ordinary share is worth £2 whether its nominal value is five new pence, one pound, ten pounds, or any other figure. This statement is only partially true—see sections on "markets" (page 11) and on "intrinsic values of shares" (page 61).

However, most American and Canadian companies have their share capital represented by shares of "no par value". Those companies with par values are in the minority.

Stamp Duty on Canadian and American Shares

In early editions of this book, nothing was said about stamp duty on share certificates in "American form" which "pass by delivery" because in most cases the stamp duty was trivial. This was changed by the Finance Act, 1963, and reference was made to it in the fifth edition (1966) although the rate of duty was still small. It was in fact so small that it was apparently not worth while collecting and it was rescinded in the Finance Act of 1967.

Dollar Premium Levy

As a result of the 1965 Budget, a seller of dollar or other designated foreign currency shares is obliged to surrender to the Exchange Control authorities the dollar premium on one-quarter of the total net proceeds. If the dollar premium at the time of the sale is 20 per cent, this means a levy of about 5 per cent, or £0·05 in £1 of the net proceeds of the sale. The broker is responsible for using one-quarter of the net proceeds to buy the necessary "investment dollars" at the ruling premium and selling them as ordinary dollars through a bank; the bank then pays the amount of the premium thus realized to the Exchange Control at the Bank of England. Since this involves a considerable amount of clerical work a charge may have to be imposed for this service.

The sale of fifty International Nickel at £21 would be worked out as follows—

		£
50 International Nickel Co. of Canada shares of no par value @ £21		1050
Contract stamp	£0·40	
Commission @ ¾%	£7·87	8·27
		£1041·73

If the dollar premium is 20 per cent, the ratio of £1041·73 to the value without the premium is 120 to 100; the value without the premium is

$$\frac{1041\cdot73 \times 100}{120} = 868\cdot1083$$

and the premium is

$$£1041\cdot7300$$
$$less \quad £868\cdot1083$$
$$173\cdot6217$$

and one quarter of this, £43·40½, has to be surrendered to the Exchange Control authorities.

Prescribed Securities

Exchange Control Regulations restrict the purchase of prescribed securities to residents in the sterling area; formerly such purchases were restricted to residents in the United Kingdom, the Channel Islands and the Isle of Man.

The main categories of prescribed securities are American and Canadian dollar securities and securities in any currency, including sterling, which are finally redeemable within five years of date of purchase.

CHAPTER V

Dividends : Delivery of Shares

THE dividend or interest is paid to all registered stock or share-holders on the same day, the dividend warrants (cheques) being posted the evening before the day on which the payment is due. Boards of directors are empowered to declare and pay interim dividends, but have to obtain the sanction of the shareholders at the annual general meeting before they can pay the final (or, if there has been no interim dividend, the only) dividend of the year on the ordinary or deferred shares. For this reason the final dividend is often paid on the day after the meeting. Some-times, if the preparation of the annual accounts has been unduly delayed, or if it is desired to pay a dividend immediately before a merger, the directors declare an interim or second interim dividend in lieu of an annual or final dividend and announce that no further dividend in respect of that particular financial year will be paid.

EX DIVIDEND

It is manifestly impossible to make out all the dividend warrants on one day, so payment is made to all holders who were registered on a specified date some time before the pay-ment is due. In the case of British Government loans the "balance is struck," to use the official phrase, on the evening of a day about six weeks before the interest payment is due and after that date all stock is transferred ex dividend.

Some companies close their transfer books for the preparation of dividend warrants for about a week but now it is usual for the books to remain open and the balance is struck on the day on which "the books close" for the dividend.

The security is made "ex dividend" on the preliminary day

next but one before the account day on or following the first or only day on which the transfer books are closed for preparation of the dividend if the Stock Exchange authorities have been notified in time or, if not, on the next preliminary day.

The prices of all securities, with the exceptions mentioned below, include all future interest or dividends until they have been made "ex" any specific payment; when a dividend is imminent or has just been declared, the price of the security may be quoted "cum dividend" (cd.) until it is made ex dividend in order to obviate misunderstandings, but this is by no means always done.

When a security is made "ex dividend" the price is adjusted by deducting the amount of the dividend (less income tax, except in cases where the dividend is paid tax free) from the "cum dividend" price.

When securities which were sold "cum dividend"[1] are delivered after the price has been made "ex dividend," then, provided the transfer books have been closed for preparation of the warrants, the buying broker is entitled on behalf of his client to deduct the net amount of the dividend from the payment due to the seller.

Suppose that on Friday, 14th May, the last day for dealing for settlement on Tuesday, 25th May, you sold the R 0·5 (£0·29) shares of a certain South African company at £0·63¾ cum the 2½p (declared sterling dividend—net amount £0·0146875) which had recently been declared and that it had been announced that, in order to prepare warrants for the payment of the dividend on 2nd July, the books would be closed from 22nd May to 1st June; the price would be made ex dividend on Monday, 17th May, so that when you delivered the shares on or after 25th May (it would be impossible to deliver earlier), the books would already have been closed and the buyer could not, therefore, be registered in time to receive the dividend from the company direct. The buyer's broker would accordingly be entitled to deduct the dividend (£0·0146875 per share net) from the purchase price. Ignoring selling expenses, you would on

---

[1] I.e. before they had been specifically made "ex dividend" since, as soon as a security is made "ex" a particular interest or dividend payment, it is automatically "cum" the next payment, although that may not be due for another six or twelve months.

delivery receive £0·6228125 per share (for the share itself without the dividend) from the buyer and the remaining £0·0146875 per share (the net amount of the dividend less tax at the provisional reduced rate of tax) would be paid to you by the company on 2nd July.

You have nothing to grumble about because you would not have had the dividend any earlier if you had kept the shares instead of selling them. The buyer, on the other hand, does in effect get the dividend earlier, since he has to pay a correspondingly smaller amount for the shares when they are delivered to him.

There is no trouble when the stock is delivered after it has been made ex dividend and the transfer books have been closed as in the example above; the buyer deducts the net amount of the dividend from the purchase price and the seller receives and retains the dividend.

Trouble does, however, often occur when the security is sold shortly before the dividend is declared and the registration of the transfers is delayed for one or other of the various reasons which so often hold up registration.

One cause of delay is the difficulty of getting the necessary signatures quickly, another is that some banks will not accept and pay for securities bought for their customers until the whole order is delivered (e.g. if the bank's customer has bought 500 shares in a company, the broker cannot deliver 400 shares that he has received from the market, but must wait till the whole 500 have been delivered to him before he can pass them on to the bank).

If shares are delivered to the buyer's broker cum dividend, but are not registered before the transfer books are closed, the broker claims the dividend for his client from the seller; in busy times, however, the making of the claim may be put on one side in favour of more urgent work, or even overlooked, until the client asks why he has not received his dividend, with the result that the seller, to his great annoyance, may receive a claim weeks after he has had the dividend (and perhaps lightheartedly spent it). The seller ought to know that he is not entitled to the dividend but few clients stop to think whether they have sold the shares cum dividend or not.

Take an instance of what may easily happen in the case of

shares in a South African company to which the Stock Transfer Act, 1963, does not apply. You sell 1,000 shares in a company when the dividend is about to be or has just been declared; "names" for 500 shares come in, 200 to be delivered to Mr. Jones of London and 300 to be delivered to the joint account of three brothers of the name of Brown who live in Manchester, Torquay and York, respectively.

The transfers are made out and posted to you the same day; you sign them, have your signature witnessed, post them back to your broker and go away for a week or ten days.

A "name" for the remaining 500 to be delivered to Mr. Smith comes in the next day, the transfer is made out and posted to you twenty-four hours after the first two transfers; you only receive it on your return home, when you sign it and send it back to your broker at once.

As soon as he got the signed transfers, your broker delivered the 200 to Mr. Jones' broker who secured Mr. Jones' signature and registered the transfer before the books closed (shares paid for "cum dividend" and the dividend eventually paid by the company direct to Mr. Jones).

Your broker also immediately delivered the 300 shares to Messrs. Brown, Brown & Brown's broker who also paid for them cum dividend; however, by the time he had secured the three signatures the books had closed, so that the company eventually paid the dividend to you (although it belonged to the Brown brothers and their broker had to claim it from you through your broker).

When at last he received the transfer for the 500 shares from you, your broker immediately delivered it to Mr. Smith's broker, but by that time the shares had been made "ex dividend" and the books were closed, so that Mr. Smith's broker deducted the net amount of the dividend when paying for the shares. (The company eventually paid the dividend to you and you were entitled to keep it.)

If you were unfamiliar with the machinery, you might well be puzzled at selling 1,000 shares in a particular company and then receiving the dividend on only 800 shares, and still more puzzled at being asked to part with the dividend on 300 of them while being allowed to keep the dividend on the remaining 500; you would, however, find on examination of the statement of your account that it had all been adjusted in the payment you received from your broker for the sale of the shares.

The price of a stock, bond or share includes the interest or dividend accrued since the last interest or dividend payment was made. If you sell a stock which is "full of dividend," you must work out for yourself how much of the proceeds represents capital and how much represents income. There are, however, certain important exceptions. U.K. Government and corporation loans with less than five years to go to the final redemption date (known as "shorts") are always dealt in plus accrued interest; that is to say, the price represents the bond alone and the buyer pays for the accrued interest separately, this being calculated to the day on which the purchase is to be settled. The buyer is not entitled to deduct income tax from the accrued interest payable to the seller as, legally, it is considered to be an adjustment of the price rather than an interest payment. During the six weeks or so after the price has been made ex dividend, interest for the number of days to the actual date of payment is deducted from the price.

"Bond washing," i.e. selling "shorts" just before the price is made ex dividend and arranging to buy them back immediately after it has been made ex dividend, is not allowed.

To recapitulate—

Bearer Securities which have to be deposited with an "Authorized Depositary" (bank, broker or solicitor) pass by delivery just like a bank-note. The main items are foreign government bonds, bearer shares (there are not many left, but one immediately thinks of British American Tobacco, Shell Transport and De Beers, which are obtainable in bearer form) and shares in "American form" which, technically speaking, are not "bearer" but "registered certificates endorsed in blank" which also pass by delivery.

Registered stocks and shares which are transferred by deed. The Stock Transfer, used for all indigenous stocks and shares, is a printed form on which only four parts are filled in before it is sent to the seller for signature—

Full name of undertaking (e.g. Courtaulds Ltd.).
Full description of security (e.g. ordinary shares of £0·25 each fully paid)

Number or amount of shares, stock or other security (shown both in words and figures).

Name(s) of registered holder(s) in full and the address if there is only one holder.

The space for the consideration money is filled in by the seller's broker after the signature(s) has (have) been obtained if all the shares mentioned in the transfer are to be transferred to one buyer. Should there be more than one buyer the document is copied on Brokers Transfers with the appropriate numbers of shares and the corresponding considerations filled in on each. The transfers are then stamped and, if necessary, certified and delivered.

The buyers' brokers are responsible for completing the transfer(s) by filling in the name(s) of the transferee(s).

In the case of securities of other countries, e.g. Australia, Kenya, South Africa (many South African companies with London registers have adopted the new Transfer system) and Zambia, use is made of the old common form of deed of transfer which is a printed form filled up as follows—

Full name(s), address(es) and description(s) of the transferor(s) (the seller or sellers).

The consideration (the money actually paid by the buyer—excluding commission, stamp duty, etc.). (Note particularly that this is seldom the same as the consideration received by the seller since there have usually been intermediate buyers and sellers.)

The full name(s), address(es) and description(s) of the transferee(s) (the buyer or buyers).

The number of shares or stock units or the amount of stock (in words and in figures) and description of the shares or stock.

The name of the company (or the title and description of the Government stock).

Below this are set out on the left the names of the people who are to sign the document; on the right are the spaces for the signatures and on the left, under the names, are spaces for the witnesses to the signatures to sign their names and fill in their addresses and descriptions. The new common form of deed of transfer is basically the same but is set out slightly differently.

There are other forms of delivery of securities which ought to be mentioned—

A number of shares in Australian and Rhodesian companies which have share registers in Australia and Rhodesia[1] only (and some which have London registers as well) are dealt in in the Stock Exchange.

In order to avoid having to send transfers to and fro it is usual to buy and sell these shares for delivery in, for example, Australia. In such cases the shares are put into the names of the nominee company of, e.g. the Australia and New Zealand Banking Group in Australia, which holds the shares to the order of the buyer's bank and sends dividends to his bank. The certificate remains in Australia and, when the holder sells his shares in London, instructions to deliver them in Australia are sent by cable. The nominee company makes a charge for its services but the buyer escapes liability to U.K. transfer stamp when he buys, and gets his money more quickly when he sells.

The shares of a growing number of European companies are dealt in in the Stock Exchange; it is the practice to have these shares, which are in bearer form, delivered in the country of origin to the correspondent (a banking firm) of the U.K. bank at which the buyer keeps his account. These shares are dealt in for cash settlement. Japanese shares can only be dealt in in multiples of 1,000. Sales of shares in companies incorporated in countries outside the sterling area are subject to the dollar premium levy. Such shares are usually identified by their par value in the currency of the country.[2]

DELIVERY

Some clients worry if the stock or shares they have bought are not delivered promptly. From the moment his broker says "Buy 500 XYZ at £1·15" and the jobber replies "Sell you 500 XYZ at £1·15" those shares belong to the buyer, and any dividend declared on them, any capitalization (or "bonus") issue and any issue made by way of rights on them, belong to him too, and if he is not registered in time to receive them direct from the company, his broker will claim them on his behalf.

[1] Dealings in Rhodesian companies are prohibited at present.

[2] Since the pound was "floated", the dollar premium is payable on shares of companies registered in Australia, New Zealand, South Africa, etc., but no levy is made on the premium when they are sold.

This cuts both ways; if you sell shares and a dividend is declared next day, the dividend belongs to the buyer and will be claimed from you.

There is one exception; when a new issue is made by open offer to shareholders or to the general public but with preferential treatment to shareholders who are given "pink forms," a buyer who has not been registered in time has to forgo the "pink form." The value of the "pink form" cannot be assessed precisely and consequently no claim can be made on the seller.

However, if the buyer had bought a really substantial amount of the security in question the chances are that arrangements could be made for the seller to use his "pink form" on the buyer's behalf.

Some companies have taken to marking the preferential forms which are issued to named shareholders with the size of the holding and taking that into consideration when making the allotments, and this eminently reasonable practice is likely to spread. If the unregistered purchase only amounted to a few hundred pounds' worth of the security, the buyer would probably miss the chance of being allotted £100 or £50 nominal of convertible debenture (or whatever the new issue might be) which he might have sold at up to 5 or even 10 points premium—the bigger the premium the smaller the probable allotment (putting the cart before the horse, in Alice Through the Looking Glass style)—i.e. he would perhaps be deprived of the chance of making a fiver. This is admittedly a real though rather trivial grievance which, like a flea-bite, is also intensely irritating.

As a result of the Stock Transfer Act, 1963, stocks and shares in companies registered in the United Kingdom are delivered more promptly than before and, as the buyer's signature is no longer necessary, purchases can be registered as soon as they are received from the market; the number of dividend claims has been reduced though not as much as had been hoped.

BUYING IN

If bearer securities bought for the account have not yet been delivered, the buyer may instruct his broker to have them "bought in" on or after the third business day after the Account

Day. If registered securities bought for the account have not yet been delivered, the buyer may instruct his broker to have them "bought in" on or after the tenth day after the Account Day.

The "buying-in" is done by a Stock Exchange official and the loss occasioned by "buying-in" is borne by the seller unless he can prove that there has been undue delay in passing the "ticket" or "name," in which case the member causing the delay is liable. When selling it is, therefore, very important to deliver the securities to your broker early enough for him to effect delivery at the proper time.

SELLING OUT

The client who has sold registered securities cannot deliver them and get his money until he has signed a deed of transfer giving the name of the transferor (the seller), the name of the transferee (the buyer), and the consideration paid by the transferee (the transfer stamp depends on the consideration paid by the transferee which is generally different from the consideration received by the transferor) has been prepared and stamped.

If the client is in urgent need of his money he should be able to get it on the Account Day even if he has to go to his brokers' office to sign the transfer.

The selling broker cannot prepare the transfer until he has received a "ticket" or "name"[1] giving the transferee's name and the consideration; if the selling broker has not received a "ticket" he may "sell out for a name" on the Friday before the Account Day, in the case of securities handled by the Settlement Department, or on the Thursday before the Account Day in the case of other securities, and any loss thereby occasioned is borne by the buyer. Since your broker cannot issue a ticket until he knows the name in which the securities are to be registered it is important that you should give him instructions as soon as you

---

[1] As a result of the Stock Transfer Act, 1963, the ticket will not give the transferee's name but only the number of shares and the price in the case of United Kingdom securities; the buying broker will issue a ticket at the proper time rather than risk having the shares sold out against him. As soon as they have been delivered to him he will register them in accordance with standing instructions.

make any purchase. This really only applies to your first purchase since, once he knows your full name, description and address, he will automatically register all purchases made for you in that name. You should, however, inform him at once if you wish any particular purchase to be registered in some other name, e.g. that of your wife, and if you normally have shares registered in the name of your bank's nominee company you should instruct your bank to accept each individual purchase from your broker and hold it for your account.

PAYMENT FOR STOCK

A broker pays his client for securities sold as soon as he has completed delivery on or after the account day, but not before, except by special arrangement. Delivery cannot be made after 1.15 p.m. and if certification is necessary (e.g. if there is a certificate for 300 shares of which 100 have to be delivered to one buyer and 200 to another) it may be physically impossible to get this done and effect delivery on the same day.

However, brokers normally pay their clients on Account Day, provided that they have a signed transfer deed in their possession, together with control of the stock (i.e. the certificate or a transfer receipt), even though they may be unable to deliver on that day.

DIVIDEND MANDATES

When clients give standing instructions for dividends to be paid direct to their bank, the broker sends a dividend mandate form to the client (usually enclosed with the contract note). This should be signed by the client and sent to the bank to be noted and returned to the broker who then registers it with the "bought" transfer. Occasionally, the bank, or the client, sends the form direct to the company's registrar, in which case it may arrive before the purchase has been registered. The registrar may then reject the form because the client is not a registered shareholder. Time might be saved if mandates were rubber-stamped "recent purchase—not yet registered".

CHAPTER VI

Orders

WHEN you approach a stockbroker for the first time it will help him to give you sound advice if you give him some idea of your age and circumstances; it is also a help if you tell him what investments you hold. Give the full description of the security as well as the amount held.

Private clients may be forgiven but banks, solicitors and accountants ought to know better than to send in ambiguous descriptions. The following composite list of items received from banks, etc., over a period of years illustrates what is meant—

British Transport 3%
There are three issues: British Transport 3 per cent 1967/72, redeemable July 1972; British Transport 3 per cent 1968/73, redeemable in April, 1973; British Transport 3 per cent 1978/88, redeemable July 1988. At the time of writing the three stocks stood at 89, $83\frac{3}{4}$, and 51 respectively.

Treasury $3\frac{1}{2}$%
There are two issues: Treasury $3\frac{1}{2}$ per cent stock 1977/80, priced at $63\frac{1}{2}$ and Treasury $3\frac{1}{2}$ per cent 1979/81, priced at 63.

Slater Walker $8\frac{1}{2}$% unsecured loan stock
There are two such loan stocks. One dated 1991/96, is priced at 83. The other is quoted either cum or ex subscription rights. It is dated 1988/93 and is priced 315 cum rights or $85\frac{1}{2}$ ex rights.

£360 Debenture and Capital Investment Trust ordinary shares £0·25 each

This turned out to be 360 shares of £0·25 each but the £ sign suggested that £360 nominal capital in £0·25 shares (i.e. 1,440 shares) might be meant.

20 Pearl Assurance

In 1958 each Pearl Assurance share of £1 was split into 4 stock units of £0·25 each; in April, 1965, these were split again into 5 ordinary stock units of £0·05 each. A list compiled from certificates kept for years in an old tin box may well show 20 shares (of £1) instead of 400 stock units of £0·05 or "20 Pearl Assurance" might mean 20 units of £0·25 instead of 100 units of £0·05. On the other hand the list may have been brought up to date and "20 Pearl Assurance" may mean 20 units of £0·05 each.

100 De Beers Cons. deferred

These may be registered (price £3·25) or bearer (price £3·35). The R 0·5 shares were split into ten shares of 5 cents in 1969. 100 de Beers Consolidated deferred may turn out to be 1,000 shares of 5 cents.

100 British American Tobacco Bearer

This might have meant 100 British American Tobacco £0·50 ordinary (£50 nominal capital) but turned out to be £100 nominal capital (200 B.A.T. £0·50 ordinary).

ORDERS

When giving your broker an order to sell, it is best to send him the stock or share certificate, or bond, with the order; you will have to send it to him eventually, so you might as well send it at once; he can then check it with your order and make sure that he is selling what you have actually got to sell—mistakes are very easily made owing to misunderstanding or to an incomplete description of the stock, and it is often an expensive matter to put them right.

When giving an order to buy or sell, give it explicitly and mention the full name of the stock or share, and the amount, and state the price at which you wish to deal or else give the order "at best" (short for "as cheaply as possible" in the case of a buying order and for "at the highest price obtainable" in the case of a selling order). Do not use Stock Exchange jargon unless you are absolutely sure of its meaning. A client once sent an order to sell "three" War $3\frac{1}{2}$ per cent, meaning three hundred pounds stock, in blissful ignorance of the fact that "three" in Stock Exchange parlance means three thousand pounds stock. Another client rang up his broker and told him to sell 200 B.S.A.; luckily the broker remembered that this particular client held no Birmingham Small Arms (often known as B.S.A.) but that he did hold 200 British South Africa Company[1] (never known as B.S.A. but usually called "Chartered") and soon verified that it was "Chartered" that the client wished to sell.

Brokers often receive letters saying that the client "would rather like" to buy this, that or the other, and have great trouble in making up their minds as to whether the letter is meant as a definite order, a discretionary order, or no order at all, but merely a request for information and advice.

It does not appear to be generally known that a broker will take an order to buy a share at a lower price (or to sell at a higher price) than the price ruling at the time the order is given, and retain the "limit"—i.e. order at a limited price, referred to as a limit for short—until executed or cancelled.

A broker will get information about a security for you and give you advice on request, without making any charge; also, if they know what your investments are, a good firm of brokers will draw your attention to it, when a sudden rise in price gives you a favourable opportunity for selling one of your holdings or exchanging it for something else.

When your broker suggests business to you, it is very important that you should reply at once, if you intend to deal, since

[1] British South Africa Company has since been merged with Central Mining and Consolidated Mines Selection in a new company called Charter Consolidated, so this particular pitfall no longer exists.

prices change from day to day, and sometimes even from minute to minute.

You may get a letter from your broker reading something like this: "The price of Flower and Reiss has risen sharply and at £0·80 we consider that they are over-valued; we suggest that you should sell your shares and re-invest in Mild and Bitters which have lagged behind in the recent rise in the brewery market and can be bought at £0·60. According to our records you hold 300 Flower and Reiss bought at £0·55 and 240 bought at £0·58¾."

He will be quite pleased if you reply "Please do as you suggest" but as he may have sent a similar letter to dozens of other clients he will have to look up the copy of his letter to you to see how many Flower and Reiss he has to sell for you.

He will be much more pleased if you write "Sell 540 Flower and Reiss" (or "Sell 700 Flower and Reiss as I already held 160 before you bought 540 for me") and "re-invest in Mild and Bitters to nearest ten shares over (or under)." He will then buy a multiple of ten shares of Mild and Bitters and know whether you wish to make or receive a small cash payment to adjust.

You may have seen in the newspapers that the price of a certain share has been fluctuating between, say, 4 and $4\frac{3}{8}$ and have decided that it was worth buying if you could get it at 4 but that you were not prepared to pay any more for it. You can give your broker a "limit" to buy so many shares at 4 limit good until cancelled, or good until such and such a date. As a matter of fact, you would be well advised to fix your limit at $4\frac{1}{64}$ or $4\frac{1}{32}$, as the chances are that a number of other people have given their brokers buying limits at the figure 4. If the share is worth buying at 4 it is also worth buying at £4·03; if you think that the extra 3p is going to turn a small profit into a loss, then it would be much better to leave it alone altogether.

You may wish to change from one investment to another (e.g. from Brass Bedsteads Ltd. $7\frac{1}{2}$ per cent preference shares into Universal Bakery Co. Ltd. ordinary shares) provided that you can get a good price for the first and buy the second sufficiently cheaply. In this case you should send your broker orders to—

sell 100 Brass Bedsteads Ltd. $7\frac{1}{2}$ per cent cumulative preference shares of £1 @ £1·07½;
buy 50 Universal Bakery £1 ordinary shares @ £2·06¼

and mark it "Contingent Order." This means that he must either execute both orders at the same time or do nothing at all.

Before June, 1966, if you sold stock or shares and re-invested the proceeds in other securities in the same or in the following account your broker could charge you reduced commission on reinvestment; the maximum reduction permissible was half of the total buying or total selling commissions, whichever was smaller. However this concession has now been abolished.

If you are going to buy a British Government stock, e.g. War Loan, you can instruct your broker to "invest" a definite sum of money in the stock; he will then buy such an amount of stock that the consideration plus commission and contract stamp add up to exactly the sum which you have told him to invest. This can be done without disadvantage since there are no transfer expenses on British Government securities. (The stock must be registered since bearer bonds are only issued for round amounts of stock.) Victory Bonds, though registered, are individual bonds, the smallest denomination being £50.

AMOUNTS TO BUY

If, however, you are buying shares it is always best to buy an "amount"—100 shares or multiples thereof if they are low-priced shares, or 50 shares or multiples thereof if they stand at a higher price—rather than odd numbers such as 37 or 42 or even 20 or 30. If you are buying several hundred shares it does not matter if you buy a few extra to bring the total cost up to the approximate amount of money which you wish to invest; if you are buying stock it is best to buy multiples of £10 stock.

The reason is that the buyer pays the transfer expenses and, though an odd number of shares can often be bought as cheaply as a round number, when you come to sell them you will probably not be able to get the full market price for them or, if you do, you will have to sell them "free" (i.e. free of transfer expenses) which comes to the same thing as accepting a lower price. These remarks apply only to registered stocks and shares.

SPLITS

Suppose that a broker is instructed to buy 1,000 shares at £1·05 for his client; if he can buy the lot from one jobber in one bargain, the consideration is £1,050, the transfer stamp is £10·50 and, as he is entitled to have the shares delivered on one deed of transfer, the registration fee at £0·12 per document is £0·12, and the total transfer expenses are £10·62. If the broker can only buy 500 at £1·05 from one jobber and has to buy the other 500 from another jobber at the same price, there are two bargains, the consideration being £525, the transfer stamp £5·50 and the fee £0·12 on each, so that, although the total consideration is still £1,050, the stamps total £11 instead of £10·50 and the fees £0·24 instead of £0·12. These are shown on the contract note and are in order. A few companies still charge a transfer fee but it is expected to disappear altogether before long.

Now, suppose the first jobber has bought 500 shares from another broker; he passes the "ticket" on to him and the 500 shares are delivered on one deed and the matter is settled. We will also suppose that the second jobber has been very unfortunate and has bought the following numbers of shares from different brokers: four separate lots of 100 each, one of 50, one of 33 and one of 17. He receives a ticket for 500 at £1·05 from the buyer and has to "split" it, i.e. he keeps the original and sends out new tickets which are exact copies except for the number of shares, the consideration (the price remains the same) and the stamp.

The buyer receives seven transfers instead of one and has to pay seven registration fees (£0·84 instead of £0·12) and £6·00 stamp, made up as under, instead of £5·50.

Number of shares	Consideration	Stamp	No. of deeds	Total stamp
	£	£		£
100	105	1·20	4	4·80
50	52·50	0·60	1	0·60
33	34·65	0·40	1	0·40
17	17·85	0·20	1	0·20
				£6·00

He is entitled to claim £0·50 (stamps) and £0·72 (registration fees) or £1·22 in all "splits" from the jobber who split the ticket. For this reason jobbers refuse to pay the full market price for small odd amounts of shares unless they happen to have a "broken book," since they know that to do so will make them liable for "splits" which, though individually small, in the aggregate amount to a considerable sum. It sometimes happens that through a ticket being split the total stamp payable comes to less than the stamp on a single transfer and in that case the client is entitled to have the saving credited to his account.

For example[1]—

the stamp on 130 shares at £1·05 (£136·50 consideration)		
is £1·50 but the stamps		
on 75 shares	(£78·75 consideration)	(£0·75 stamp)
and 55 shares	(£57·75 consideration)	(£0·50 stamp)
total 130 shares	(£136·50 consideration)	£1·25

a saving of £0·25 stamp less £0·12 extra registration fee, or £0·12 net.

When buying bearer shares (or units of stock in bearer form) it is also best to buy a round number since there is usually a plentiful supply of bearer warrants for 100 shares (or 100 units) but a shortage of warrants for 50, 10, 5 or single shares and you have either to pay a little extra for these or else to wait a long time for delivery, although, when you come to sell them, the chances are that you will not be able to get anything extra for them.

American and Canadian shares are usually dealt in in multiples of ten; certificates for smaller numbers of shares can be obtained but it is hardly worth the trouble to do so except, of course, in the case of shares standing at very high prices.

Investors with a small amount of money to invest, say £200 or so, often hesitate to buy "heavy" shares standing at £8, £10 or more for the £1 share, and seem to think that they have less chance of making a profit by so doing than they would have by buying shares the price of which is about the same as the nominal value.

[1] This example is no longer true, as the stamp duty rates were altered in August 1970.

HIGH-PRICED SHARES

Many businesses have built up positions of enormous financial strength over a long period of years, and have gradually increased their dividends; their shares have gradually risen in price and these high prices are a measure of the confidence felt in the companies concerned by the investing public. Provided that the yield obtainable on the money invested is not too small and that the company is known still to be pursuing a conservative financial policy, such shares provide a safer investment than that provided by the lower-priced shares of companies which have not got such a good financial record.

It is true that the speculator often does better with shares of which he can afford to buy a round hundred, but the small investor, who intends to hold his shares more or less permanently, should not be frightened of buying a few high-priced shares; he may have to give away something in the price when he comes to sell them again, although this is not usually the case if the consideration is over £100.

Until recently the commission scales made it much more expensive to invest the same amount of money in low-priced shares, but that has been changed and a flat rate of 1¼ per cent on the money is now charged. All the same it is, on the whole, more expensive to invest in low-priced than in high-priced shares because of the jobber's turn; the size of this depends on a large number of factors which are discussed on another page, but as an example it would not be surprising to find a difference of ½p between the prices at which you could buy or sell shares standing at £0·07½ (6·6 per cent) while the corresponding differences for shares standing at £3·40 and £5·75 might be 2p and 2½p (0·59 per cent and 0·44 per cent respectively).

STOP-LOSS ORDERS

On the day of the general election a broker received an order, in force for that day only, to buy a certain number of shares at £0·87½; so far, so good. However, the letter went on, "if the price falls after you have bought the shares, sell them at £0·82½ and so limit my loss to a shilling." Now a few minutes' reflection will show that no broker can accept an order like that; when is the broker to sell? Normally there may be a $\frac{1}{2}$p price in the shares (i.e. they can be sold at $\frac{1}{2}$p less than the price at which they can be bought) but, if news is received which is sufficiently bad to cause the price of a share standing at £0·87$\frac{1}{2}$ to drop 5p in the course of an hour or two, the chances are that there will be sellers only and no buyers, or at the best the price will be widened considerably (i.e. there will be a margin of 1p, 2p or more between the prices at which the shares can be bought and sold, instead of only $\frac{1}{2}$p). If the price falls and widens from £0·87–£0·87$\frac{1}{2}$ to £0·82$\frac{1}{2}$–£0·85, the broker may consider it his duty to sell hurriedly at £0·82$\frac{1}{2}$ while he can and then, if the price rises again, his client may be annoyed at his having sold the shares at £0·82$\frac{1}{2}$ when the middle price was still as high as £0·83$\frac{3}{4}$; on the other hand, if he waits to see what is going to happen, he may find that within a very few minutes the price has fallen to £0·80–£0·85 with "nothing inside" (i.e. no buyer to be found above £0·80 and no seller below £0·85). A broker cannot accept an order of this kind without placing himself in an impossible position.

If a client wishes to give a "stop loss" order, he must tell his broker to sell "at best" as soon as the shares are offered at a given price. In this instance he would probably instruct his broker to sell at best as soon as the shares were offered at £0·83$\frac{3}{4}$; he would then have a good chance of getting out at £0·82$\frac{1}{2}$ or, at any rate, at £0·81$\frac{1}{4}$.

VALUATIONS

Owing to the recent spate of take-over bids and mergers, in addition to the splitting of shares sometimes combined with a capitalization issue, brokers must exercise great caution when preparing valuations because the lists submitted to them may be out of date.

Some of the traps encountered were shown at the beginning of this Chapter, others most likely to occur are listed below— "100 Australia and New Zealand Bank" may turn out to be 135 Australia and New Zealand Banking Group, the Company formed on the merger between Australia and New Zealand Bank and English, Scottish and Australia Bank.

"300 British Insulated Callenders Cables" may turn out to

be 800 B.I.C.C. £0·50 ordinary shares since the £1 shares were split into 2 of £0·50 followed by a 1 for 3 capitalization.

"500 General Engineering" may be either 500 General Engineering (Radcliffe) Ltd., £0·10 ordinary shares, or 500 General & Engineering Industries Ltd., £0·20 ordinary shares.

The only safe course is to check the holding with the Registrar of the company concerned.

When preparing a valuation for probate, the solicitor concerned will be grateful if the broker points out the companies which are incorporated in countries other than England. In such cases the executors cannot dispose of the shares until the grant of probate has been "re-sealed" in Scotland or registered with the High Commissioner or Ambassador of the country concerned. Burmah Oil, Distillers and General Accident Fire & Life Assurance are the three Scottish companies which immediately come to mind in this connection; companies incorporated in other countries are readily identified by the currencies in which the face value of the shares is expressed; shares of no par value are almost certainly American or Canadian.

When preparing a valuation for probate, the net amount of the dividend (after deduction of tax at the standard rate) has to be added if the price was made ex dividend before the date of death and the dividend was paid afterwards. This is because the value of the dividend does not appear in the price (which is ex dividend) and does not appear in the deceased's bank account at the date of death, as it has not yet been paid. The interest on $3\frac{1}{2}$ per cent War Loan is paid gross and must be added to the valuation gross.

When a death occurs on a Saturday, Sunday, or any other day when the Stock Exchange is closed, the valuation for probate may be prepared using prices from the Stock Exchange Official List of the business day immediately preceding, or immediately following, the date of death. However, all the prices need no longer refer to the same day.

The price used for probate purposes is taken from the Stock Exchange Daily Official List and is generally taken as "one quarter of the spread added to the bid price." Thus an Official List price of £1·25–£1·30 has a spread of 5p so that $1\frac{1}{4}$p is added to £1·25 to make a probate price of £1·26$\frac{1}{4}$.

CHAPTER VII

Share Values

INTRINSIC VALUE OF SHARES

IT is an extremely difficult matter to estimate the intrinsic value of a share, since so many things have to be taken into consideration. The novice should consult his broker before making his choice of an investment, but it is just as well that he should know something about the matter himself as he will otherwise be unable to appreciate the broker's remarks.

A high yield suggests that the shares are rather speculative, but it may indicate that there is very little market, so that if he buys the shares he may find it difficult to sell them again.

He should remember, too, that a mine is a wasting asset; a mining share, when considered as an investment rather than a gamble—there are mining shares which can be considered as sound investments—should offer a sufficiently high yield to enable him to regard part of the dividend as a reasonable rate of interest on the money invested and the rest as a return of capital. The mode of division between income and return of capital depends on the estimated life of the mine—that is, the number of years expected to elapse before the mine is worked out. A brickworks also comes into this category, since the supply of clay in the brickfields will not last for ever.

In considering debentures or preference shares he should discuss the cover available, while, if he turns his attention to ordinary shares, he must see how much is left (the equity) after providing for the prior charges (debentures and preference shares).

He must also, of course, consider the prospects of the industry in which the company is engaged, the state of trade in the districts which it supplies, the elasticity of the demand for its products or services, and the strength of the competition.

VALUATION OF ASSETS

It is, of course, impossible to calculate the exact value of the equity of a company; "goodwill" may be of great value to a company as long as it continues to trade but, as it is an intangible asset, many well-managed concerns take no credit for it, either omitting it from the balance sheet altogether or putting it among the assets at the nominal figure of £1. Office furniture is indispensable and may appear among the assets at cost, less depreciation; this is perfectly legitimate, but if the company went into liquidation it might be found impossible to sell the office furniture except at a rubbish price; and so on with all the other assets except cash, debtors (after providing for bad and doubtful debts) and gilt-edged investments.

Since the end of the Second World War the purchasing power of the pound has fallen considerably, with the result that assets such as freehold land may now be worth four or five times as many pounds as they cost fifty or sixty years ago. Some companies have had their properties revalued fairly recently and have capitalized a large part of the increase in the balance sheet and distributed fully-paid new shares to the ordinary shareholders in proportion to their holdings.

Obviously a firm cannot afford to have its properties revalued very often but, if it does not do so, the actual capital employed in the business may be seriously understated, so that the ratio of earnings to capital employed looks much better than it really is and prevents shareholders from realizing that the board of directors is not doing as well as it might. This is the kind of situation that inspires an astute business man to make a take-over bid, since he is clever enough to see that the assets, if properly managed, can be made to bring in much bigger returns. Such take-over bids are not necessarily entirely good or bad. The shareholders get cash or shares in another company to a value greater than that of their shares before the date of the bid; the employees of the company taken over may or may not get a fair deal; some or all of the directors may get a cash payment as compensation for loss of office ("the golden handshake") which seems an astonishing reward for having failed to make the best use of the company's assets. On the other hand, it is not easy to draw the line between the take-over of a wealthy company with a moribund management and the merger on a share-exchange basis of a large and a small company which are both well managed but which can make substantial savings in management and manufacturing expenses by combining.

In fact, the value to be assigned to the various assets depends on whether one is discussing their value to the company as a going concern or what they would fetch if the company went into liquidation.

One may hear a man say that the ordinary shares of Whatnot Ltd. stand at £1·75 but that, as the company is a flourishing concern and as the "break-up" value of the share is £1·60, they must be cheap. He means that, in his opinion, if the company were wound up, the tangible assets could be sold to provide enough cash to pay off the company's debentures and other liabilities, to repay the preference capital in full and leave enough to distribute £1·60 per share to the ordinary share-holders; his contention therefore is that a man who buys the ordinary shares at £1·75 is paying £1·60 for real assets and only £0·15 per share for the earning capacity of the company.

Again, it must be remembered that it may or may not be legitimate to value a company's holding in a subsidiary company of 100,000 shares whose market price is £3, at £300,000. The dividend paid on these shares may be sufficient to provide a handsome return on a capital of £300,000 and from this point of view they may justifiably be valued at this figure, but if cash were wanted in a hurry, the chances are that the sale of only 10,000 of these shares would lower the price very considerably. These remarks lead up to a discussion of balance sheets and the information which can be obtained from them, which hardly comes within the scope of this little book.

GEARING

One often reads of companies with a high- or low-geared capital; what is meant can best be explained by means of two hypothetical examples.

Consider first of all a company with this capital structure—

Loan Capital		Annual Interest
5½% 1st Debenture	£100,000	£5,500
6½% 2nd „	£100,000	£6,500

	Share Capital	*Annual Interest*
7% Preference Shares	£500,000	£35,000

Total annual requirement for prior charges £47,000

Ordinary Shares	£200,000

Suppose that after providing for depreciation, bad debts, and corporation tax of 45 per cent, the net profit were £50,000, then, after paying the prior charges (£47,000), a dividend of 1½ per cent could be paid on the ordinary shares. If the next year the net profit were doubled (at £100,000) there would be £53,000 available for the ordinary shares, a sum equal to 26½ per cent on the ordinary share capital; i.e. doubling the profit would enable the ordinary dividend to be multiplied by 17⅔—a high-geared company.

Now consider a company with this capital structure—

	Loan Capital	*Annual Interest*
	None.	None.
	Share Capital	
6% Preference Shares	£100,000	£6,000

Total annual requirement for prior charges £6,000

Ordinary Shares	£800,000

Suppose that after providing for depreciation, etc., the net profit were £50,000, it would be possible to pay a dividend of 5½ per cent on the ordinary shares (costing £44,000). If in the following year the net profit were doubled (at £100,000) there would be £94,000 available for the ordinary shares, which is equivalent to a dividend of 11¾ per cent; that is, doubling the profit would barely do more than enable the ordinary dividend to be doubled—a low-geared company.

Conversely, the halving of the net profit would, in the case of the company with the low-geared capital structure, be likely to lead to the halving of the ordinary dividend, while, in the case of the high-geared company, it would lead, not only to the passing of the ordinary dividend, but to the passing of the preference dividend as well. (When a dividend is not paid it is said to be "passed.")

Thus it is evident that, other things being equal, the shares of a high-geared company are more speculative than those of a low-geared company.

Companies with a high-geared capital structure are also described as "top-heavy." The bulk of the capital has been subscribed by the preference shareholders, who take most of the risk, while the ordinary shareholders (who may have put up none of the capital but received their shares as consideration for the goodwill of the business) take most of the profit, if things go well.

PRIORITY PERCENTAGES AND EARNINGS COVER[1]

As an illustration of what is meant by these terms and to show how misleading "earnings cover" can be in an extreme case, consider two companies which both show a profit of £100,000. (The profits and dividends in these two examples are net figures after deduction of tax.)

The capital of Company "A" consists of a large amount of first preference shares, a small amount of second preference shares and the rest in ordinary shares (dividend £30,000 in this particular year).

The capital of Company "B" consists of a medium amount of preference shares and the rest in ordinary shares (dividend £40,000 in this particular year).

	1st Pref.	2nd Pref.	Ordinary	Reserves and increased carry forward
Company "A"				
Net dividends	40,000	5,000	30,000	25,000
Profit left after paying the dividend	60,000	55,000	25,000	
Times covered by earnings	2·5	12·0	1·83	
Priority percentages	0–40	41–45	46–75	76–100
Company "B"				
Net dividends	20,000		40,000	40,000
Profit left	80,000		40,000	
Times covered	5·0		2·0	
Priority percentages	0–20		21–60	61–100

[1] The Finance Act 1972 radically changes these calculations—see Addendum, page 183.

In the case of Company "A", although the first preference dividend is covered only $2\frac{1}{2}$ times, the second preference dividend is covered 12 times, which is, to say the least, misleading. The priority percentages give a much clearer and more straightforward picture. Occasionally you find the priority percentages going over 100 per cent, e.g. 81–105 per cent; this represents an over-allocation of the year's profits and a reduction, instead of an increase, of the "carry forward."

The foregoing has been over-simplified since no account has been taken of investment allowances or of the great variation in different industries of the proportion of earnings which must necessarily be retained in the business to finance expansion, and which consequently are not available for distribution of dividends. It must also be remembered that, in times of rising prices, replacement costs are much greater than original costs and that amounts allocated to depreciation are rarely adequate, quite apart from the fact that new machinery is often more complicated and, therefore, more expensive than the obsolescent machinery which it replaces.

Owing to the different systems of tax collection in different countries, comparison of earnings of companies in the same type of business, but in different countries, may be misleading.

Under the tax system in force before the Finance Act, 1965, it was customary to show priority percentages with reference to net profits after tax; it could hardly be calculated otherwise as, although the company paid tax on the whole of its profits, it was allowed to retain the income tax deducted from dividends; this made no difference to the total tax paid by the company and its shareholders, but the bigger the dividend, the more tax was paid by the shareholders and the less by the company itself. It remains to be seen how priority percentages will generally be shown in future.

Below are shown the priority percentages worked out on the old system and then under corporation tax at 35 per cent and at 45 per cent to see how they compare. In the first instance interest and dividend distributions are shown net, in the other two they are shown gross; although income tax will have to be deducted from them it will be paid direct to the Inland Revenue and will not appear in the company's accounts except as contra entries.

The company chosen as an example had £2,237,500 6 per cent Loan Stock outstanding and an issued capital consisting of £1,320,000 7 per cent preference and £3,226,500 ordinary shares. The trading profit was £951,700 after deducting expenses, but before tax, and £440,161 after deducting income tax at £0·38¾ and profits tax at £0·15.

	Loan Interest	Corporation Tax	7% Pref.	Ordinary (12½% gross)	Increase (+) or decrease (−) in carry forward	Total earnings (£s)
Old system	82,228 net % 0–18¾	—	56,595 net % 18¾–31½	247,028 net % 31½–87¾	(+)54,310 % 87¾–100	440,161
Corporation Tax at 35%	134,250 gross % 0–14	286,107* % 14–44	92,400 gross % 44–53⅞	403,312 gross % 53⅞–96¼	(+)35,631 % 96¼–100	951,700
Corporation Tax at 45%	134,250 gross % 0–14	367,852* % 14–52⅝	92,400 gross % 52⅝–62⅜	403,312 gross % 62⅜–104¾	(−)46,114 over-allocation of 4¾%	951,700

* On £817,450 (£951,700 less £134,250 gross loan interest).

CHAPTER VIII

New Issues

As a result of the Companies Act, 1947, subscription lists may not be opened until the third day after publication of the prospectus. This gives time for intending applicants to consult their financial advisers and to read the newspapers' comments on the issue before applying, besides giving investors outside London an equal chance of securing an allotment.

ISSUE AND ALLOTMENT

As the lists for a successful issue close within a minute or two of their being open, applications must be posted in time to arrive by first post on the day on which the lists open. Since applications may be withdrawn after the expiration of the third day after the opening of the subscription lists (Saturdays, Sundays and Bank Holidays being disregarded in counting the days) the Issuing Houses try to get the allotments and letters of regret posted as quickly as possible. On the other hand, applications have recently been accompanied by dud cheques and, in order to weed these out, issuing houses now often announce that all cheques accompanying applications may be presented for payment, and this is bound to cause some delay.

Fixing the price of a new issue is a very difficult matter; any company that is expanding is likely to want to raise fresh money sooner or later, and this will be much easier if the first or the most recent issue has been a success; to ensure this the price of the issue must be made attractive without giving too much away.

It is wise for the beginner to apply only for what he is willing to take up and pay for in full, as he may otherwise be landed with a nasty loss. In September, 1969, a certain new issue was subscribed sixteen times over and yet, when dealings started, the price was between £0·05 and £0·07½ below the issue price.

The basis of allotment when an issue has been heavily over-subscribed is often criticized. Sometimes it is decided to allot 100 shares to all those applying for, say between 100 and 5,000 shares and scale down heavily all the big applications; this is done so as to obtain a large and diversified body of shareholders; sometimes all the small applications are ruled out and the large applications are only moderately scaled down, in order to keep down the expense of handling the issue and of issuing future dividend warrants.

When an issue is particularly heavily over-subscribed the only solution is to ballot for allotment and issue 100 shares each in respect of applications for up to 500, 1,000 or even 5,000 shares which are lucky in the ballot, and to scale down all the bigger applications very heavily. Sometimes issues of shares are made by tender, and for certain types of company this may well be repeated; this method is particularly suitable where it is difficult to assess future profits, as in the case of a property development company. In one case a quarter of a million shares were offered for sale at a minimum price of £0·80, applications to be for multiples of 100 shares at £0·80 or any higher price which was a multiple of £0·02½. Allotments were to be made at the highest price at which the offer was fully subscribed; applications at higher prices were to be accepted in priority to applications at lower prices, subject to certain qualifications. In deciding the basis of allotment, consideration was to be given to the desirability of spreading the shares over a reasonable number of applicants in relation to the number of shares offered, the size of the company and the desirability of obtaining a Stock Exchange quotation and of establishing a market in the shares. In fact, the issue was over-subscribed three and a half times at prices ranging from £0·80 up to £2.

All the shares were allotted at £0·87½, this being the highest price at which the offer was fully subscribed and which ensured that no one applicant obtained a huge allotment. The issuing house obtained £0·07½ per share more for their clients than they would have received if the issue had been made at £0·80 in the ordinary way, the allotments were reasonably well spread and the "stags" were kept at bay. The stags are those who apply for a new issue in the hope of obtaining an allotment which they can sell at once at a profit; since they only apply for issues which they expect to be heavily over-subscribed, they habitually apply for far more shares than they are able to pay for, so if the issue turns out to be a flop and they get a full allotment, they have to sell at once and take a heavy loss.

It is impossible to please everybody. If the small applicants are cut out, the little man is being unfairly treated; if the little man is favoured, the jobbers complain of the trickle of tiny sales and the brokers resent the volume of unremunerative work entailed. If the issue is made by tender—probably the fairest method—the financial press complains that it is the job of the issuing house and the broker to the company to fix the issue price; they are well paid and ought not to shirk their responsibility and leave the small investor to guess the price at which he should tender. Of course, he can get this advice from his broker and from the financial columns of the daily newspapers.

The real drawback to "stagging" is that if all goes well you only receive a small allotment or no allotment at all, whereas, if it goes badly, you get all you have applied for. One bad issue can wipe out the profit on half a dozen successful efforts and it must be remembered that, however good the company, the issue can turn out to be a failure because of some happening quite unconnected with it, for example, fresh trouble in the Middle East, the crash of an airliner, the assassination of a politician, or a strike at home.

When a company is too small to warrant the expense of an offer for sale, the shares are sometimes put on the market by way of a "placing"; the Stock Exchange Council dislike this method because it is virtually impossible to give the general public a fair chance of participating, and it is only allowed when no suitable alternative can be found.

In the case of a "placing" the jobbers who are going to deal in the shares accept applications for shares from brokers at the placing price; if too many applications are received they either scale them down or ballot for them. The jobbers inform the brokers a day or two before dealings start how many shares have been allotted to them, subject to permission to deal, or that they have been unlucky in the ballot, and the brokers apportion them to their clients as fairly as they can. "Names" have to be passed immediately so that only the original buyers get shares registered in their names free of transfer expenses.

PARTLY-PAID SHARES

When new shares are issued to the public a small amount is usually payable on application, a further small instalment on allotment (if the issue is over-subscribed an applicant will only be allotted a proportion of the amount applied for; the amount of his remittance left over after paying the application money on the shares allotted to him is used in paying the instalment due on allotment, and the balance, if any, returned to him) and the balance is payable in two or three instalments due on definite dates spread over some months.

Formerly it was usual to issue shares of fairly large denomination and to "call up" only a small proportion of the nominal amount of each share; the balance could be called up in whole or in part by the company at any time and was thus a liability to the shareholder.

The company could refuse to register a man as a shareholder of partly-paid shares if they thought he was a "man of straw" who might be unable to meet a call.

Partly-paid shares are a liability to the holder but they give confidence to creditors of the company since, if it is in difficulties, it can call up extra capital.

Partly-paid shares are obsolescent; in the past banks and insurance companies formed the chief classes of concern in which partly-paid shares were common, on account of the extra confidence which it gave to their creditors, but these companies have built up such impregnable financial strength that this is no longer necessary, and most of them have reorganized their capital and now only have fully-paid shares.

Hambros Bank Ltd. has £10 shares, £2·50 paid but the unpaid £7·50 is what is known as the "Reserve Liability"; that is to say that the holder of these shares can only be called upon to pay £7·50 per share in the event of a winding-up and this is unthinkable. The marketable shares of this company are, however, the £0·25 fully paid shares.

All the same, most nominee companies will refuse to have

partly-paid shares registered in their names, on account of the liability.

This does not apply to new issues which are to become fully paid in the course of a few weeks, provided the beneficial owner puts the nominee company in funds to pay the calls as they fall due.

Apart from offers for sale, etc., mentioned above, there are two other kinds of new issues.

CAPITALIZATION ISSUE

When a company has built up a large reserve account by ploughing a large part of the profits back into the business, or has a large share-premium account, or a recent valuation of its land and buildings has shown them to be worth very considerably more than the figure at which they formerly stood in the balance sheet, it may decide to capitalize a part or all of these reserves in order to bring the issued capital more nearly into line with the actual capital employed in the business.

This may be done in a number of different ways. If the issued capital is in the form of £1 shares, £0·25 paid, the reserve may be used to extinguish part or all of the liability and to make the shares £1 shares, £0·75 paid or fully paid. Alternatively, after increasing the authorized capital (if this is necessary) it may issue new shares credited as fully paid to existing shareholders in proportion to their holdings in whatever proportion is convenient; e.g. one new share for every share held, one for two, three for five or even four for one.

This is usually done by issuing fully-paid renounceable allotment letters to the shareholders; these new shares are transferable free of transfer expenses (no transfer stamp and no registration fee) for a short time (usually about three weeks). The seller merely signs the "Renunciation Form" (usually marked "Form X" on the back of a allotment letter) and the buyer's broker completes a "Registration Request Form" (usually marked "Form Y") and has it registered before the final renunciation date. If the original shareholder does nothing it does not matter, since the new shares are automatically registered in his name.

When shareholders receive these fully-paid allotment letters they often sell them at once under the erroneous impression that they have received something for nothing. In the case of a one-for-one scrip bonus they have, in effect, merely received two 50 pence coins for a pound, since the price of the shares would be halved on the day on which the price of the old shares was made "ex capitalization." That, of course, is not quite the full story, as the shareholders do, in fact, get several benefits.

In the case of a one-for-one scrip bonus the number of shares is doubled, so that they become more marketable. The price is halved so that a number of investors who would not dream of buying a share standing at, say, £6 cheerfully come into the market to buy them at £3 and the price rises more rapidly than it would otherwise have done.

Other investors buy the new shares because they are free of stamp and fee, without pausing to reflect that the price of the new shares in the form of "letters" usually stands at roughly the value of the stamp over the price of the old (registered) shares; in other words, the cost of buying new shares is usually almost the same as that of buying the old, the only difference being that the value of the stamp goes to the seller of new shares instead of being paid to the Inland Revenue in the form of stamp duty. The real benefit to the shareholder lies in the fact that a scrip bonus is often the prelude to a larger amount of cash being distributed as dividend; that is to say, if a company paid 27½ per cent before the one-for-one scrip bonus, the same amount of cash distributed as dividend would result in a 13¾ per cent dividend on twice as many shares, but one would expect a dividend of, say, 15 per cent or more after the bonus, subject to any dividend limitation.

A recent innovation introduced by Bowater Paper, and rapidly followed by the Beaver Trust, was to make a capitalization issue by means of renounceable certificates instead of fully-paid allotment letters. This method saves an enormous amount of work since, instead of issuing definitive certificates in exchange for all the allotment letters, definitive certificates only have to be prepared and issued to replace those which have been renounced.

Fully-paid allotment letters (and provisional allotment letters—see below) and renounceable certificates can be "split" until shortly (usually two days) before the final renunciation date.

If you have a renounceable allotment letter or certificate for, say, 450 shares and wish to keep part and sell the rest (or give them to somebody), you sign the renunciation form and send the document to your broker with your instructions (e.g. to split it so that you can keep 200, give 150 to your wife and sell 100); he will take it to the company or the issuing house handling the issue and will receive in exchange three "split" allotment letters or renounceable certificates still in your name but rubber-stamped "split letter (or certificate)—original duly renounced"; the 200 are in your name so nothing need be done about them; your wife's name and address are filled in on the split letter (or certificate) for 150 by your broker, who has it registered, and the 100 are delivered to the market. A charge of £0·05 per split allotment letter or certificate is no longer made.

Another method which is rather unpopular among share-holders was once adopted by Shell Transport when they made a one-for-five scrip issue; the price was made "ex capital-ization" and a few weeks later certificates (not renounceable) for the new stock units were posted to shareholders.

The prices of the old and new shares can be calculated quite easily provided you remember that the value of the old shares "cum capitalization" is the same as that of the old shares "ex capitalization" plus that of the new shares.

For example, in a three-for-five capitalization, if the old shares stood at £4·50, five shares were worth £22·50 before the issue and £22·50 is the value of eight shares after the issue; you would expect the old to stand at

$$\frac{£22·50}{8} = £2·81\tfrac{1}{4}$$

ex capitalization, and the new at £2·81¼ plus the value of the stamp (say 2¾p) or £2·84, but, as market conditions change continually, that would only be a guide.

Since these scrip bonuses spring largely from profits ploughed back into the business, the *Daily Express* coined the neat term "ploughshares" to describe them.

Fractions. Fractions of shares are not issued; it is usual for the shares left over, i.e. all the fractions added together, to be allotted to an officer of the company as nominee and for him to sell them in the market and to distribute the net proceeds to the shareholders entitled to them. Thus, in the example above, a shareholder with 101 shares would be entitled to 60⅗ shares; he would receive 60 new shares and a cash payment in respect of the fraction; if the surplus shares were sold at £2·85 (about £2·81¼ after deducting commission) the cash payment would be £1·68½.

RIGHTS ISSUES

When a company needs to raise fresh money it often does so by giving holders of ordinary shares or stock the right to subscribe for new shares in proportion to their existing holdings, at a price below the market price for the old shares (but not below the face or par value, since it is illegal to issue shares at a discount except in special circumstances and then only by permission of the Court).

The issue is made by posting to each shareholder a Provisional Allotment Letter stating the name and address of the shareholder (mentioning joint shareholders, if any), the number of shares held, the number of new shares provisionally allotted (fractions ignored) and details which should be studied very carefully; it is usual to mark the envelope "Not a Circular" and to print on the top of the Provisional Allotment Letter words to the effect that "This is a valuable document and if you do not understand it you should consult your stockbroker or banker immediately."

Sometimes the whole issue price has to be paid on acceptance; sometimes it is payable in instalments a few weeks apart. The important point to notice is that, if the acceptance payment is not made by the date specified, the rights lapse. Some directors take the view that, if the shareholder cannot take the trouble to look after his rights by taking them up or selling them to somebody else who wishes to do so, he deserves to lose them; in such cases the Provisional Allotment Letter is accompanied by a "Form of Application for Excess Shares," the excess shares being those not taken up by the shareholders entitled to them and the surplus shares arising from fractions; application forms of this kind are made out in the name of the shareholder and can be used by him only.

Other directors feel that their shareholders should be protected against their own carelessness, which may not be carelessness at all (the allotment letter may go astray in the post or the shareholder be too ill to attend to business), and they sell any shares not taken up and distribute the proceeds to those entitled to them.

A broker received two or three days after the last day for acceptance a Provisional Allotment Letter duly renounced, with instructions to sell it. When he pointed out that the rights had expired before the Letter had even been posted to him the client wrote indignantly that the last day for renunciation was still over two weeks ahead!

It must be emphasized that the rights lapse if they are not accepted by making the proper payment by the date specified; the new shares are dealt in "nil paid" until the day before payment is due, and are then dealt in, still in the form of renounceable letters fully paid, for a further period which is usually three weeks. In some cases, when the amount due is payable in instalments, they are dealt in "partly paid" for an intermediate period.

Formerly the buyer of new shares had to sign the "Registration Application" form on the renunciation letter when it had been delivered, but under the Stock Transfer Act, 1963, this is no longer necessary; the buyer's broker merely fills in the buyer's name and address and registers it with the company.

Almost all allotment and provisional allotment letters are renounceable but occasionally a company making a capitalization issue merely issues new share or stock certificates or issues non-renounceable allotment letters, which are merely temporary certificates and are transferable only by deed subject to stamp duty.

As mistakes are easily made and are often costly to put right, two warnings may be made here.

1. In respect of capitalization issues it is becoming common to issue fully-paid allotment letters which state that if they have not been renounced they may be exchanged for definitive certificates on or soon after a certain date, e.g. 22nd September, but that if they have not been so exchanged by, say, the end of October they will become valueless and the relative certificate will be sent to the shareholder by post.

This is a dangerous practice, since few people take the trouble to read documents carefully; the probable result will be that Mr. A, receiving such an allotment letter, will say "I needn't bother to do anything about that as the certificate will be posted to me" and put the allotment letter away in his desk. A few months later he will receive the certificate and send it to his bank for safe keeping, and a year or two later he will sell the whole of his holding in that particular company. Years later still, he (or his executors) will find the allotment letter and, without reading it carefully, cheerfully sell the shares mentioned therein, only to find that the allotment letter had become valueless years before and that he or they have sold shares that they no longer possess.

2. A company, with its issued ordinary capital in the form of stock transferable in units of £0·25 and its authorized but unissued ordinary capital in the form of £1 shares, decided to capitalize reserves and issue one £1 share for every £4 stock, the new shares being converted on allotment into stock transferable in units of £0·25.

This was taken as a 25 per cent or one-in-four capitalization issue, and so it was—more or less; to be accurate it was a four-for-sixteen issue, which is very nearly, but not quite, the same thing.

At first sight the holder of 1,000 units would expect to get 250 new units, and the danger is that a year or two later he might say "I think I'd better sell my holding in that company; yes, I remember I had 1,000 and I got a one-in-four bonus—I'll ring up my broker and tell him to sell 1,250."

In fact, he held 1,000 units of £0·25, which was £250 stock; he received one share of £1 for every £4 stock, i.e. 62 new shares which then became 248 units of £0·25 each and his total holding after the issue was not 1,250 but 1,248 units. This looks as if the brokers to the company had failed to see the implications or had been unable to persuade the secretary to the company that there was a neater way of executing the Board's wishes.

Had the £1 shares been subdivided into shares of £0·25, and one new share of £0·25 issued for every £1 stock held and then converted into stock, this snag could have been avoided. So look at your allotment letters very carefully before you sell them.

Letter of Rights or Subscription Warrant. When a Canadian company, particularly a bank, issues new shares by way of rights it does not issue a provisional allotment letter but a letter of rights or subscription warrant entitling the shareholder to subscribe for so many new shares and fractions of shares. Fractions cannot be taken up but the fraction can be made up to a whole share by buying the necessary fraction.

Valuation of Rights. The price of a share is normally made "ex rights" on the day on which shareholders receive their Provisional Allotment Letters. At the moment of being made "ex rights" the value of the old shares plus the new money to be put up equals the value of the old shares (ex rights) plus the new shares (fully paid).

For example: 1 new share offered at £0·50 for every 8 shares held, the old shares standing at £0·80.

$$8 \text{ shares @ } £0\cdot80 \text{ plus } £0\cdot50 \text{ (cash)} = £6\cdot40 + £0\cdot50 = £6\cdot90$$

$$= 9 \text{ shares in all @ } \frac{£0\cdot690}{9} = £0\cdot76\tfrac{2}{3}$$

The rights would be worth £0·80 less £0·76⅔ or 3⅓p per old share. The price would be £0·76½ "ex rights" and the new shares (nil paid but with £0·50 to pay) would be £0·26½ premium; since the new shares would temporarily be free of stamp duty to a buyer the premium would be slightly more than £0·26½.

RAISING MONEY

Fashions change in methods of raising money as in everything else. Not long ago companies took to issuing redeemable preference shares but these now seem to have gone out of fashion.

There was a time when convertible debentures were extremely popular as they enable the holder to "sit on the fence," at any rate for three or four years. They are the usual fixed-interest bearing loan redeemable in fifteen or twenty years' time, but for the first three or four years the holder is entitled to convert each £100 debenture stock into a certain number of ordinary shares; the number of ordinary shares obtainable for £100 debenture stock diminishes slightly each year and is so calculated that, if the debenture stock is taken at the issue price, the cost of the ordinary shares obtained by conversion at the first conversion date is slightly higher than the price of the ordinary ruling at the time of the announcement of the convertible debenture issue, and slightly higher still at each subsequent conversion date.

The debenture may be converted once a year at a certain date on the terms announced and, after the final conversion date, the debenture stock becomes a plain fixed-interest bearing stock.

Since the issue of a convertible debenture stock may result in the issue of ordinary shares at below the market price, it is usual to offer such stock only to ordinary shareholders in the company: the size of the shareholding will usually be considered in making the allotments if the issue is over-subscribed.

The dates shown are the first date on which the company may redeem the stock and the date by which it must redeem the stock, just as with a "straight" debenture or loan.

What is not shown in the description of the stock is of much greater importance, for example—

(a) The dates on which holders may convert into ordinary shares

(b) The terms on which they may convert; in some cases these become progressively less favourable, in others they remain the same throughout the years until the conversion rights expire. More recently convertible loans or debenture stocks have been issued with conversion rights which become more favourable as time goes on.

(c) The right which in many cases the company concerned reserves, either to redeem, or to convert all outstanding convertible stock the moment that holders of a certain (very large) percentage of the stock have converted.

A good example of a convertible stock issued by way of rights to ordinary shareholders is Dunlop 7¾ per cent convertible unsecured loan stock, 1989/94, which was offered to ordinary shareholders in 1966 at 100 per cent.

Each £100 stock was convertible into 74 ordinary shares in May, 1969, into 69 shares in May, 1970, or into 64 shares in May, 1971. To one who subscribed for £100 stock at par (100) the cost of the ordinary shares would be

$$\frac{£100}{74} = £1 \cdot 36\tfrac{1}{2}$$

if he converted in 1969; £1·45 if he converted in 1970 and £1·56¼ if he converted in 1971.

If he bought the stock at 107 which was the price at the time of writing, the equivalent prices on conversion would be £1·55 in 1970 and £1·67 in 1971. As the market price of the ordinary shares is £1·51¼, it can be seen that the convertible stands at a premium of $2\frac{1}{2}$ per cent over the price of the ordinary shares. At 107 the convertible yields 7·25 per cent, whereas, the ordinary shares yield only 5·27 per cent. When the final conversion date has passed any stock left unconverted will revert to being solely an unsecured loan stock and the price will drop so that the yield falls in line with the "going" interest rates. In this case the price would fall to about 83 to yield 9·35 per cent.

If you consider that a $7\frac{3}{4}$ per cent unsecured loan stock of this nature is worth 83, and you bought the stock at 107, you would, in effect, have paid 83 for the loan stock and 24 per cent for the right to choose in 7 months' time to have 69 ordinary shares instead of £100 loan stock. That works out at £$\frac{24}{69}$ or £0·34$\frac{3}{4}$.

The rules of the Stock Exchange only allow option dealings for three months ahead, and the three months' call on Dunlop ordinary shares at £1·51$\frac{1}{4}$ might well be about £0·17$\frac{1}{2}$. It can be said that the convertible stock offers a seven month option at £0·34$\frac{3}{4}$.

A more recent variation of convertible stocks is the unsecured loan stock with subscription rights. Here, a holder may subscribe for ordinary shares on specified dates at fixed prices, on the basis of a fixed number of shares for every £100 stock held. The primary differences between these stocks and convertibles is that, after the rights have been exercised, you still hold a loan stock and, secondly, you have to pay for the shares to which you are entitled.

STERLING DOLLAR CONVERTIBLES

An American Company wishing to take over a U.K. company is not allowed simply to offer its own dollar shares in exchange for U.K. sterling shares. If this were to be done the shareholder would be obliged to sell his shares to the company and to buy investment dollars (dollars including the dollar premium) in order to pay for the American shares. These complications, and capital gains tax considerations, make this normally out of the question. If the bidder does not wish to offer cash, then the solution is a sterling convertible loan stock, convertible at a later date (sometimes in over ten years' time) into the common shares of the parent company. On conversion, the holder surrenders his stock to the U.K. agent of the company who will issue the appropriate number of common shares to him. The agent will satisfy the Exchange Control regulations by purchasing premium dollars in the investment currency market and by selling them in the official currency market. Until conversion, the stock remains a sterling investment.

WHAT TO READ

There is, unfortunately, no short cut to financial knowledge nor is it easy for the beginner to read financial articles and understand what the writer is driving at, since many of the expressions used, and still more the ideas underlying them, are unfamiliar. Most of the daily papers have a financial article and it is fair to say that its reliability and soundness of view is probably of much the same standing as that of the rest of the paper. *The Financial Times*, as might be expected from its title, gives a service which at present is unique in publishing daily the highest and lowest prices for the year, the present price, dividend, dividend cover and yield of a very large number of stocks and shares. If you like a financial article written from an unusual angle and with a sense of humour, George Schwartz in *The Sunday Times* should have most appeal.

It is instructive to read the chairman's speech at the annual general meetings of important companies, such as the "Big Four" banks, Imperial Chemical Industries, Shell, Boots Pure Drug, Marks & Spencer, and Woolworth and plenty of others. Sir Halford Reddish, until recently the Chairman of Rugby Portland Cement, usually made a speech that was well worth reading; these meetings are reported in the City pages of the daily press and a rough idea of their importance may be obtained from the amount of space devoted to them. Then there are the weeklies such as *The Economist*, the *Investors Chronicle* and *The Statist*. It is also a good plan to read books on "How to Read a Balance Sheet" and similar subjects. This book is deliberately somewhat elementary; those who want something more advanced should read M. S. Rix's *Investment Arithmetic*.

From time to time the journalists suggest that the Stock Exchange ought to publish not only the prices at which business has been done but also the number of shares which have been dealt in. In this country stockbrokers do their business by "minding their own business"; large transactions often take several days to complete and would probably never be done at all if the prices and number of shares dealt in had to be published. The size of many Stock Exchange transactions would stagger the man in the street if he knew about them; they are only possible because, being the private concern of the principals, they are kept private.

British and American Capitalization Issues

When a United Kingdom company makes a "one for one" capitalization issue, the shareholder keeps his share certificate and receives from the company a new certificate for the same number of shares.

When an American company makes a "two-for-one stock split" (which comes to the same thing) the shareholder surrenders his certificates to the company and receives new certificates for twice the number of shares.

CHAPTER IX

Trustee Securities

TRUSTEES are by law only allowed to invest in certain securities unless the Trust Deed explicitly gives them wider powers of investment; some Trust Deeds allow the trustees to retain non-trustee securities but not to invest in such securities; in such cases, if these securities are sold, the proceeds must be re-invested in trustee securities.

It is not criminal for trustees to invest in non-trustee securities but, if they do so, the beneficiaries under the trust may sue them for any loss incurred by their so doing. Not only that but, if the trustees invest in two non-trustee securities and make a profit on one and a loss on the other, the beneficiaries of the Trust are entitled to take the profit on the one and sue for the loss on the other; the trustees may not set off the profit against the loss.

Under the Trustee Act, 1925, a trustee was empowered to invest in a long list of fixed-interest bearing stocks including all British Government and British Government Guaranteed stocks and a number of Dominion and Colonial Government stocks and United Kingdom municipal and county stocks. Provided he invested in a "Trustee Stock" he could not be attacked, however disastrous the results.

Under the Trustee Investments Act, 1961, a trustee is empowered to have the trust funds valued and divided into two equal parts on the basis of that valuation; after that, one part must be invested in "Narrower Range" securities and the other part may be invested in "Wider Range" securities. A very important point is that, except as explained below, the trustee is obliged by law to obtain professional advice although he is not compelled to act on that advice. The wording of the Act is "proper advice is the advice of a person who is reasonably believed by the trustee to be qualified by his ability in and practical experience of financial matters," which presumably means an accountant, banker, or stockbroker.

The curious thing about the 1961 Act is that there does not appear to be any legal obligation for a trustee to obtain advice until he has decided to divide the fund into "Narrower Range" and "Wider Range" sections, and that this decision may be indefinitely postponed, but a trustee who failed to seek advice would clearly lay himself open to severe criticism. Even after he has had the trust fund valued and divided, he is entitled to invest the money in Defence Bonds or National Savings Certificates or by depositing it with the Post Office Savings Bank or other bank deposit account without advice. Money in both sections of the trust fund may be invested in "Narrower Range" securities but only money in the "Wider Range" section may be invested in "Wider Range" securities.

The valuation must be made professionally, and the professional advice about investments in either range, except as above, must be obtained or confirmed in writing unless one or two or more trustees is himself the professional adviser, in which case it appears that the Act does not require the advice to be in writing. The intention of the Act appears to be to make it obligatory for a trustee to consider the advisability of spreading the funds over different industries and over different companies in those industries, taking into account their suitability for the purposes of the Trust. It also makes it obligatory for a trustee to review the holdings at suitable intervals.

Stocks and shares which were not trustee securities under the Trustee Act, 1925, held under special powers, e.g. a trustee empowered to retain although not empowered to invest in such securities, are to be excluded from the valuation made prior to dividing the trust funds into "Narrower Range" and "Wider Range" parts. Such securities are to be carried to a separate part of the fund. If such securities are subsequently sold the proceeds are to be divided equally between the "Narrower Range" and "Wider Range" parts of the Trust Fund. The "Special Range" also includes land.

As it is obligatory for trustees to take professional advice there is no point in doing more here than to indicate the type of security in which they are allowed to invest under the Act.

Narrower-Range Investments (Not Requiring Advice)

Part I. Defence Bonds, National Savings Certificates and deposits in the Post Office Savings Bank.

Narrower-Range Investments (Requiring Advice) Part II.

British Government Securities

Securities issued and registered in the United Kingdom by the government of any overseas territory in the British Commonwealth.

Local-authority securities registered in the United Kingdom and quoted on a recognized stock exchange.

Debentures or debenture stocks of a company incorporated in the United Kingdom, of which the total issued and paid-up share capital is not less than one million pounds and which has paid a dividend on all the issued shares in each of the five years immediately preceding the calendar year in which the investment is made.

Loan stocks, whether secured on assets or not, of such companies.

Deposits in an approved building society.

Mortgages on freehold property or leasehold property with not less than sixty years' lease unexpired at the time of investment.

Perpetual rent-charges charged on land in England, Wales or Northern Ireland and in feu-duties in Scotland.

There is one equity in the Narrower Range; curiously enough, it is the stock of the Bank of Ireland, which was incorporated by Royal Charter in 1783. The dividend is 20 per cent, the price range for 1968/69 (October) was £4·00 to £9·00 and the latest price is £4·50. The market in this stock tends to dry up at times, but there is a reasonable market at present.

Wider-Range Investments (Requiring Advice)

Any security authorized in the Narrower Range, Parts I and II.

Any fully-paid securities issued and registered in the United Kingdom by a company incorporated (by Charter or under the Companies Act) in the United Kingdom of which the total issued and paid-up share capital is not less than one million pounds and which has paid a dividend on all the issued shares in each of the five years immediately preceding the calendar year in which the investment is made.

Shares or debenture stock must be fully paid up except for new issues, which are required to be fully paid up within nine months of the date of issue.

An issue of new shares which, by their terms of issue, do not rank for the dividend for that year, does not exclude a company from trustee status.

A company formed to take over the business or to acquire the securities of, or control of, another company or other companies, shall be deemed to have paid a dividend in any year in which such a dividend has been paid by the other company or all the other companies.

Shares in an approved building society.

Unit trusts authorized by the Board of Trade.

Trustees must consider the purposes for which a trust has been made and try to hold an even balance between the claims of the life tenants and of the remaindermen in selecting their investments. They must also consider buying dated stocks to mature at times when beneficiaries are due to receive their share of the capital absolutely at known dates (on attaining specified ages) or at unknown dates (marriage) at which an intelligent guess may perhaps be made.

TRUSTEES AND THE CAPITAL GAINS TAX

1. When a person sets up a trust, all the property which he gives to the trust is deemed to be disposed of by him at the market price at the time. The person setting up the trust is liable for capital gains tax just as if he had sold the securities (or other property) in the market.

2. Trust funds are liable for capital gains tax arising on the sale when a change of investment is made, and losses can be carried forward to be set off against future profits. The trustees are responsible for declaring the profit and for paying the tax out of trust funds.

3. When a beneficiary becomes absolutely entitled to part or all of the funds of a trust (e.g. on attaining the age mentioned in

the trust deed), the trustees are deemed to have disposed of the securities to the beneficiary at the market prices on the relevant date. If there is a net gain over

(a) value at market prices when the settlor set up the trust

(b) value at Budget Day prices

(c) the cost of the securities

(whichever is relevant) the trustees must pay capital gains tax, selling part of the securities if necessary to raise the cash for that purpose before transferring the residue to the beneficiary. If there is a capital loss which cannot be deducted from gains realized in that year of assessment, the beneficiary is allowed to carry the loss forward to set off against future profits made by him.

4. If a life tenant continues to survive, the securities need not be valued and gains declared for capital gains tax until his death.

5. At the death of a life tenant, if one or more beneficiaries become absolutely entitled to all or part of the securities, the securities to be transferred absolutely are valued for capital gains tax, presumably at probate prices, as in (3) above except that there is a £5,000 relief to be apportioned between the aggregated personal estate and trust funds.

6. When at the death of a life tenant, he is succeeded in part or *in toto* by another life tenant, the trust funds other than those to be transferred absolutely as in (5) above, are exempt from valuation for capital gains tax provided that such a valuation has been made within fifteen years, but such a valuation must be made at the end of fifteen years from the previous valuation. No further valuation is required until the death of the second life tenant, and then only if fifteen years or more have elapsed since the previous valuation. A valuation may be necessary for estate duty but where one life tenant is succeeded by another within fifteen years of the previous valuation for capital gains tax, this is not regarded as a "disposal" and consequently no charge to capital gains tax arises.

7. In the case of a trust where there is no life tenant, e.g. a discretionary trust, valuations for capital gains tax must be

made every fifteen years. In the case of a trust made before 6th April, 1965, the first valuation must be made at the expiry of fifteen or of a multiple of fifteen years from the first date when there was no life tenant, but the first valuation is not to be made before 7th April, 1967.

CHAPTER X

Yield on Securities

"YIELD" is a term which is continually cropping up and it may be as well to explain its meaning here. Briefly, the yield on any particular security means the annual income obtained on an investment of £100 in that security.

CALCULATION OF YIELD

The important thing is to distinguish between the rate of interest or dividend paid on the loan or share and the rate received on the money invested in it. Thus £5 is paid every year on each £100 nominal of a 5 per cent stock; the holder of £100 stock receives £5 a year, irrespective of what he paid for the stock. If he paid £100 cash for his £100 stock, the yield is 5 per cent; if, however, it only cost him £80 cash, he is getting £5 income for each £80 invested, which is equivalent to £6¼ per £100 cash invested, i.e. the yield is 6¼ per cent.

Suppose a pound share pays 5 per cent dividend and can be bought for a pound; the yield is 5 per cent; a pound share which pays 10 per cent and which can be bought for two pounds also yields 5 per cent on the money, and so do pound shares which pay 2½ per cent and which can be bought for fifty new pence, and twenty-five new pence shares which pay 15 per cent and can be bought for seventy-five new pence.

This is only strictly true if the share is bought the day after the dividend has been deducted from the price, i.e. when the share has just been made ex dividend, for at any other time the price of the share includes part of the dividend for the current year which has "accrued" although it has not yet been declared (assuming that a dividend is being earned and will be declared in due course), and thus the yield on the money is somewhat higher than the result indicated by the rough and ready method of calculation used above.

In practice the yield is usually calculated as indicated above, simply by multiplying the interest or dividend rate by the nominal or face value of the stock or share and dividing by the purchase price, since the result is sufficiently accurate for purposes of comparison.

For example, a $3\frac{1}{2}$ per cent stock that can be bought at $53\frac{5}{8}$ yields

$$\frac{3 \cdot 5 \times 100}{53 \cdot 625} = 6 \cdot 526(8)\%, \text{ say, } 6\frac{1}{2} \text{ per cent;}$$

a £1 share paying 20 per cent that can be bought at £3·92½ yields

$$\frac{20 \times 1 \cdot 00}{3 \cdot 925} = 5 \cdot 095(5)\%, \text{ say, } 5 \text{ per cent;}$$

a £0·20 share paying 10 per cent that can be bought at £0·42½ yields

$$\frac{10 \times 0 \cdot 20}{0 \cdot 425} = 4 \cdot 705(8)\%, \text{ say, } 4\frac{3}{4} \text{ per cent.}$$

Some people find difficulty in working out the yield on a share of no par value. By definition the yield is the annual income from the investment of £100, so, if the income and the amount invested are known, the yield can be found by simple arithmetic. Shares of no par value are either American or Canadian so the important thing is to make sure that price and dividend are in the same units; if you work on a dividend in U.S.A. dollars and a price in sterling without converting the dollars to sterling, the answer will be meaningless.

For example, Canadian Pacific $25 shares pay $3·10 (Canadian) annual dividend, and the price is £54 in London. The Exchange Rate is $2·57 Canadian = £1, so $1 Canadian is roughly £0·39. Therefore an investment of £54 produces an income of $3·10 Canadian (approximately £1·21).

An investment of £100 would produce an income of

$$\frac{£1 \cdot 21 \times £100}{£54} = £2 \cdot 23$$

or, in other words, the yield is 2·23 per cent.

Sometimes it is necessary to work out the yield much more accurately taking into account not only the expenses but also the accrued interest or dividend (assuming that the previous year's dividend rate will be maintained).

As examples, let us work out Ruritania 6 per cent bonds with two months' accrued interest in the price and Commercial Co. Ltd. £1 ordinary (registered) on which 12 per cent has been paid once a year for some years and which can be bought at £1·60 with five months' accrued dividend.

In each case assume that sufficient is bought for us to consider the ordinary rates of commission; if only a small amount is purchased, the broker has to charge minimum commission, which is out of all proportion.

COMPARING EXPENSES

Suppose that the client buys £1,000 Ruritania 6 per cent; the contract will be as follows—

	£
£1,000 Ruritania 6% (bearer) @ 80	800
Contract stamp	0·20
Commission ½% on consideration	4
	£804·20

As two months' interest (= 1% less tax @ 41¼ per cent = £0·58¾) is included in the price, we can consider the actual cost to be £804·20 less 1% (less tax) of the nominal amount (= £5·87½), that is, £798·32½. The annual gross income, 6 per cent on £1,000, is £60, so that we can now calculate the yield on the money invested thus—

$$£60 \text{ on } £798·32\tfrac{1}{2}$$
$$? \text{ on } £100$$

$$= \frac{60 \times 100}{798·325} = £7·5167\% \text{ or approximately } 7·51\tfrac{5}{8}\%$$

The same client also buys 480 Commercial Co. Ltd.; the contract will read—

	£
480 Commercial Co. Ltd.	
£1 ordinary shares @ £1·60	768·00
Contract stamp	0·20
Transfer stamp	8·00
Registration fee	
Commission 1¼% (money)	9·60
	£785·80

As five months' dividend = 5 per cent less tax @ 41¼ per cent = £2·93¾ per cent on £480 nominal = £14·10 is included in the price, we can consider the actual cost to be £771·82½, so that we can now calculate the yield on the money invested (12 per cent on £480 = £57·60) thus—

$$\frac{£57·60 \times 100}{771·825} = 7·463\%$$

Of course there is no point in working out the yield exactly unless you are considering the investment of a large sum of money; if you have £200 to invest, you do not really mind whether it will bring you in £11·12½ or £11·429, though you want to know whether it will bring in £10 or £12.

The yield, however, is of importance, even when investing a small sum, since it is a guide to probable price movements; if the shares of one company offer a higher yield than the average for shares in companies of the same class, it is worth while inquiring why. It may be that unfavourable developments are anticipated, in which case it is safest to leave it alone, but the price may have been depressed by the liquidation of a deceased estate, in which case it is reasonable to expect it to rise until the yield has fallen to the average, when the liquidation has been completed.

YIELD WITH REDEMPTION

When buying British Government stocks, Foreign Government bonds, or debentures, which have a definite redemption date—the redemption date is the date on which the borrower is obliged, by the terms of the loan, to pay back the loan against delivery of the bonds which are then said to be redeemed— allowance must be made for yield "with redemption." Unless the redemption date is fairly remote, the current price is not likely to be more than a few points above the redemption price (in which case there will be a loss on redemption) but stocks can often be bought considerably below the redemption price.

When a loan has two dates as part of its title it means that the borrower may redeem the whole loan at any time after the first date, on giving due notice, and must redeem the whole loan not later than the second date, e.g. Exchequer 5 per cent Loan 1976/8, which the Government may redeem on 26th September, 1976, and must redeem at 100 on 26th September, 1978 at latest. You must look out for two words "or after" in the title of a loan; "War $3\frac{1}{2}$ per cent 1952 or after" may be redeemed at any time but need never be paid off; "Treasury $2\frac{1}{2}$ per cent 1975 or after" may not be redeemed (at 100) until 1975 and that, too, may never be redeemed. "Conversion $3\frac{1}{2}$ per cent 1969" had to be paid off at 100 on 1st March, 1969, but "Conversion $3\frac{1}{2}$ per cent 1961 or after" has no final date.

When a Government loan falls due for redemption a new loan is usually issued to raise the money and holders of the stock to be paid off are often given the opportunity to convert into the new loan.

When money is cheap, i.e. it can be borrowed at a low rate of interest, the Government tries to issue long-dated loans so as to pay the low rate for as long as possible, but in view of the fate of "Daltons," as Treasury $2\frac{1}{2}$ per cent, 1975 or after, is known, which now stand at about $28\frac{1}{2}$, it is unlikely that the Government will ever again be able to issue a loan without a definite final redemption date. When money is dear, if the Government has to borrow, it does so for a comparatively short term in the hope that a cheap money period between the first and last redemption dates will enable it to pay the loan off and raise a new or conversion loan at a lower rate of interest.

Companies raise loans which are known as debentures, or debenture stocks if secured on the general assets of the company, or as mortgage debentures if secured on specific assets; many of the very big companies enjoy sufficiently good credit to be able to issue unsecured loan stocks. These usually have two redemption dates and are often repayable for two or three years after the first date at two or three points premium, then for a year or two at a lower premium and at the final date at par (100).

Many debentures are redeemable by means of a sinking fund (the company must under the terms of the issue spend a fixed sum annually on redeeming the debenture stock or must redeem a fixed percentage of the stock still outstanding); in some cases the debenture stock may be bought in the market if obtainable at or under par plus accrued interest; if not so obtainable, stock is "drawn" (by ballot) for redemption at par. In some cases the company is not entitled to buy stock for the sinking fund in the market but must draw stock for redemption at par or at a small premium. Some debentures are irredeemable.

Capital gains in the hands of private individuals used not to be subject to any tax, whereas income is subject to income tax and surtax; a man with an income of over £15,000 derived from investments pays 91¼ per cent (41¼ per cent income tax and 50 per cent surtax) on the top slice. This is where redemption yields become interesting and the most important field is in the gilt-edged market. Whereas other Stock Exchange securities are subject to capital gains tax, British Funds were exempted in the 1969 Finance Act provided that they had been held for at least twelve months before sale or the redemption date. Net redemption yields on low coupon stocks thus became attractive to surtax payers. Two stocks taken from a gilt-edged investment list at the time of writing illustrate what is meant. When making calculations of this kind, redemption at the latest possible date is always assumed if the market price is below the redemption price of 100 and the earliest possible date if the price is above par.

Savings 3 per cent Bonds 1965/75 must be paid off at 100 on the 15th August, 1975, at the latest. In December, 1969, they could be bought at 77¾. At this price the flat, or running yield, is £3·87 per cent.

$$\frac{3 \times 100}{77\cdot75} = 3\cdot87(2)\%$$

In this case, as the stock has to be paid off at 100 in just about 5¾ years' time, there is a capital profit on redemption of 22¼ points (not $22\frac{1}{4}$ per cent but $22\frac{1}{4}$ per $77\frac{3}{4}$) which is 28·75 per cent on the purchase price, or 5 per cent per annum.

$$\frac{28\cdot75}{5\cdot75} = 5\cdot0$$

This makes the yield, allowing for redemption at 100 in 1975, 3·87 plus 5 = 8·87 per cent as a rough approximation; in fact, the yield is not as much as this since £100 in five and three quarter years' time is not worth as much as £100 cash now.

The formula for working out the redemption yield is—

$$\text{Redemption yield} = \text{flat yield} + \frac{(RP - PP)\dfrac{r}{100}}{\left(1 + \dfrac{r}{100}\right)^{n} - 1}$$

where RP = redemption price
      PP = purchase price
       r = rate per annum
       n = number of years to redemption.

As the leading gilt-edged jobbers issue daily investment lists giving prices, flat yields and gross and net redemption yields, it is far less trouble to ask your broker to get one of these lists for you or to give you particulars of the stock in which you are interested.

In practice, the figures in these lists are calculated by the conventional procedure of finding, by trial and error, the unique rate at which the sum of the present values of the redemption proceeds and the annuity represented by the interest payments equals the price, and then adjusting for small variations in the price.

The redemption yield on Savings 3 per cent Bonds 1965/75 at $77\frac{3}{4}$ in December, 1969, was shown on one of these lists at £8·22 per cent. Now, of that £8·22 per cent, £3·908 is taxable income and £4·312 per cent is a tax free gain. (It is, in a sense, only notional since you do not receive a penny of the capital gain until the redemption date if you hold the stock to maturity; on the other hand, your stock must rise in price as the period to the redemption date gets shorter as, otherwise, the redemption yield would become very large.) £3·908 less tax at 41·25 per cent is £2·296, so the net redemption yield is £2·296 plus

£4·312 (flat yield less tax plus the redemption portion of the yield) = £6·608.

Gross this up at 41·25 per cent tax; £1 less tax at 41·25 per cent is 58¾p; 'grossing up' reverses this process so that 58¾p after tax becomes £1 before tax; £6·608 after tax becomes

$$\frac{£6·608}{£0·5875} = £11·24(8) \text{ per cent gross.}$$

That is to say that, if you pay tax at the standard rate, by buying Savings 3 per cent Bonds 1965/75 at 77¾ in December, 1969, and holding it to redemption at 100 in 1975 you would have received the equivalent of having invested your money at a flat yield of 11·2 per cent, all of which would have been subject to tax at 41¼ per cent. If you were a surtax payer the attraction of the stock would be even greater since you would "gross up" at a higher rate (income tax plus surtax) but of course the net annual income would be smaller as surtax as well as income tax would have to be deducted.

Savings 3 per cent was fairly short-dated and in August, 1970, having then only five years to final redemption had become "a short" dealt in at a price not including accrued interest, which is calculated separately. When a stock becomes "a short" the price usually rises, since discount houses and similar institutions can then buy it for purposes for which only "shorts" are eligible.

Now, take a long dated stock, Treasury 9 per cent 1994, which has to be paid off at 100 on 17th November 1994; this can be bought at 96⅞ to yield 9·29 per cent flat; the 3⅛ points of capital appreciation are spread over twenty-five years so the redemption yield is only 9·43 per cent and the net redemption yield 5·59 per cent but, in this case, practically the whole of the yield consists of taxable income.

The surtax payer must look for a low coupon loan with a comparatively short date ("coupon" is used as an abbreviation for "interest rate"). When Government loans were obtainable in bearer form each bond had a number of coupons attached; these had to be cut off (French "couper," to cut) and presented for payment at the due date. For example, a £100 bond bearing interest at 5 per cent would have coupons worth £2·50 each, bearing dates at six-monthly intervals.

The Finance Bill originally sought to impose a tax on all

capital gains. However, after protest that this was tantamount to redeeming Government Loans at prices arbitrarily fixed at levels below the contractual redemption price, the Chancellor of the Exchequer conceded to the extent of declaring free of capital gains tax all profits made by buying Government stocks at or above the lowest issue price of that security and selling (or having the stock redeemed at maturity) at or below 100.

The concession was extended by the Finance Act, 1969, to free all U.K. Government stocks held for over twelve months from capital gains tax.

TAXATION RELIEF

While on the subject of yields, something must be said about taxation. All companies registered in the United Kingdom are required by law to deduct income tax at the standard rate (41·25 per cent) from dividends and to issue with the dividend warrant a "tax voucher" which states that tax has been deducted and has been, or will be, paid to the proper authority and that the Inland Revenue will accept the voucher as a certificate that tax has been deducted. With income tax at 41·25 per cent there is no difference between a dividend of 58¾ per cent tax free and one of £1 less tax. However, if company A has paid 58¾ per cent tax free for some years and continues to do so after the standard rate has been raised to, say, 42½ per cent, the shareholder will still receive 58¾ per cent after tax but will have to declare

$$\frac{58\frac{3}{4} \times 100}{57\frac{1}{2}} = £1\cdot02$$

gross while, if company B still pays £1 less tax, the shareholder in that company will still have to declare £1 gross dividend but will only receive £0·57½. Similarly, if income tax were reduced to 37½ per cent, the "A" shareholder would receive £0·58¾ net or £0·94 gross, while the "B" shareholder would receive a gross dividend of £1, amounting to £0·62½ net.

People who derive the whole of their income from investments have tax deducted at standard rate at source on all of that income. As the first slice of a person's income is not liable to tax, and the second slice is taxable at reduced rates, such people pay more tax than the amount for which they are liable and they must claim repayment of the amount overpaid. The Inland Revenue make such repayments very promptly but may only do so out of taxes which they have themselves received.

ALTERNATIVE REDEMPTION YIELD

There appears to be no satisfactory formula for calculating a redemption yield; the formula on page 95 is complicated and a simpler formula follows which gives a reasonably accurate result, providing that the term is not too long or the premium or discount too large.

$$\text{Redemption yield} = \frac{100(nc+d)}{100n - \dfrac{nd}{2} - \dfrac{d}{4}} \text{ or } \frac{100(nc-p)}{100n + \dfrac{np}{2} + \dfrac{p}{4}}$$

where n = number of years to redemption

    c = coupon rate

    d = discount

    p = premium.

CHAPTER XI

Taxation

TAXATION is a complicated subject mainly outside the scope of this book but, as it affects investment policy, some aspects of it must be considered here, particularly in relation to the Finance Act, 1965.

CAPITAL GAINS TAX

The method of computation of capital gains is the same for individuals and companies but gains in the hands of individuals are assessed to capital gains tax while gains in the hands of companies with certain exceptions are assessed to corporation tax.

One feature common to both short-term and long-term capital gains tax, is the Budget Day, 1965, price; this is defined as whichever is higher, the middle of the Official Quotation or half-way between the highest and lowest prices at which bargains done on 6th April, 1965, were marked (i.e. "marks" in the Official List of 6th April excluding business done on the previous day and "marks" in the Official List of 7th April noted as referring to the previous day). Marks at special prices are excluded. The Stock Exchange has published an Official List of 1965 Budget Day prices for easy reference.

The price has to be adjusted for rights or capitalization issues in the same way as the market dealing price. Also, adjustments must be made for capital distributions and, of course, if shares are received as a result of a take-over, an adjusted price must be calculated. These adjustments can be complicated and the Exchange Telegraph Company publishes a book showing both the crude and adjusted prices; as this book is used by the Inland Revenue, their calculations can be relied upon.

In cases where securities were acquired before Budget Day, 1965, at prices below Budget Day prices and subsequently disposed of at a profit, the profit liable to tax is to be computed as though they had been acquired at Budget Day prices, and the rest of the profit is not liable to tax.

Similarly, if securities were acquired before Budget Day, 1965, at prices above Budget Day prices and subsequently disposed of at a loss, the loss available to be set off against profits for the purpose of computing capital gains tax, is to be computed as though the securities had been acquired at Budget Day prices and the rest of the loss is to be disregarded.

In the case of securities bought and sold in the market, dealing expenses are to be taken into account in calculating the profit or loss: dollar premium on purchase and surrender to Exchange Control of part (at present $\frac{1}{4}$) of the dollar premium on sale of the securities are part of the dealing expenses.

In the case of securities acquired before Budget Day at prices above Budget Day prices and subsequently disposed of at a loss at prices above Budget Day prices, there may be some difficulty in convincing H.M. Inspector of Taxes that there was no taxable gain unless the purchase contracts can be produced.

Contracts were often thrown away after certificates for the purchases had been received or the money had been paid against delivery of the securities sold. On account of capital gains tax all purchase and sale contracts should be carefully preserved.

Short-term Capital Gains Tax, 1965[1]

This replaced the 1962 short-term capital gains tax. It does not apply to limited companies but only to "individuals", though the term includes joint accounts, trustees and limited companies such as bank executor and trustee companies acting as trustees. Under this tax all profits resulting from the disposal of securities within twelve months of their acquisition are assessable to income tax and surtax as if they formed the top slice of unearned income.

Short-term losses can be set off against short-term gains or carried forward indefinitely for that purpose, but they cannot be set off against anything else.

[1] The 1971 Finance Act abolished short-term Capital Gains Tax and all gains are now taxed at the same rate of 30 per cent.

Capital Gains Tax (formerly known as "Long-Term")

This is a thinly-disguised capital levy since no allowance is made for the erosion of the purchasing power of the pound. There will be many cases where the tax is levied on paper profits which in terms of real wealth are actually losses.

All capital gains made by limited companies, irrespective of the time for which the securities have been held, are chargeable to corporation tax.

The long-term capital gains tax applies to capital gains made by "individuals" on securities held for more than twelve months. The taxpayer has the choice of paying 30 per cent of the whole of the net profit or of having half of the net profit (up to a maximum of £5,000 in one fiscal year with marginal relief for profits slightly exceeding that figure) assessed to income tax and surtax as the top slice of unearned income and keeping the other half of the profit tax free.

If an individual's total sales for any one fiscal year do not exceed £500 in value, there is no liability to Capital Gains Tax on any profit that has been made.

Investment trusts[1] and unit trusts[1] are obliged by law to provide capital gains tax vouchers similar to the familiar income tax vouchers which are attached to dividend warrants; shareholders can use these vouchers as credits to set off against their personal capital gains tax liability on selling these particular shares or units at a profit.

Disposal of securities. In addition to sales in the market gifts *inter vivos* are regarded as a disposal of assets and create a capital gains tax liability to the donor or a loss for him to set off against profits as though the securities had been sold at market price.

The death of a shareholder is regarded as a disposal of the shares at the probate price and will create a capital gains tax liability on the estate. In this connection there are two concessions[2]—(1) no capital gains tax will be levied if the total gain on the whole estate does not exceed £5,000, and (2) any capital

---

[1] The 1972 Finance Act made such trusts liable only to 15 per cent Capital Gains Tax and they no longer issue vouchers.

[2] Capital Gains Tax on a deceased estate has been abolished because the Inland Revenue lost in Estate Duty what it gained in Capital Gains Tax.

gains tax incurred will be allowed as a deduction from the estate before assessment to estate duty.

Capital gains tax has left its mark in a number of ways. Speculative investors who see a profit on their shares will tend to hold on until twelve months have elapsed, thus helping to raise prices still further; before this tax was introduced, profit taking had a greater tendency to slow down the pace of any rise.

This can be illustrated by an investor (or perhaps one should say speculator) who bought 100 Poseidon shares at £5 each costing, say, £500. After three months and a phenomenal rise in price, his holding became 100 shares at £100 valued at £10,000; if he were to sell, his profit of £9,500 would become only £2,018·75 after surtax and income tax at 78¾ per cent. He would suffer heavily for having £9,500 of unearned income and any other income he might have would also become liable to surtax. If he held on until a year elapsed, he would only be liable to long term capital gains tax of 30 per cent, and his net profit would be £6,650 assuming, of course, that the price was still £100. However, even if it were halved to £50, his net profit would be £3,150 which still compares favourably with £2,018·75, his net profit on sale at twice the price after short term tax.

At one time it was considered sound advice to cut a loss if the price started dropping, but many speculative investors hung on in the hope that the price would improve. With capital gains tax in mind, they are encouraged to cut the loss within twelve months in order to reap the tax benefit and falls in price can, accordingly, become exaggerated. In the past, rapid rises in price were checked by "bear" selling. This was largely confined to experienced operators, mostly the "big boys" who are heavy surtax payers; these are the people who suffer most from short term gains tax and, as the bulk of any profit they make will disappear in income tax and surtax, they are reluctant to take big risks for very small net profits. There is, therefore, less check on unwarranted rises in price.

Similarly, in the absence of "bear" closing on sudden and heavy falls, these can be exaggerated by the new tax.

The effect that frequently occurs is that prices fluctuate much more widely than in the past; this may provide a happy hunting ground for the speculator which is, presumably, the last thing that any government really wants.

In addition, it is a corollary that the flow of sales and purchases are impeded to the detriment of the genuine investor who has to pay more for his purchases and get less for his sales than he would have done had this tax not been introduced.

Where many different factors are at work, it is impossible with any certainty to apportion effects to individual causes. There is no doubt that markets are narrower than they used to be; that is to say that one could formerly deal in a larger number of shares at a closer price than is possible at present and there is little doubt that the short-term capital gains tax, 1962, and its successors, the 1965 short-term and long-term capital taxes, constitute one important cause of this state of affairs.

CORPORATION TAX

The formation of companies with limited liability enabled capital to be raised for large projects such as the building of a railway, since, for the first time, it became possible for an individual to subscribe a definite part of the required capital, however large or small, without incurring any liability, should the enterprise fail, beyond the loss of the amount subscribed.

A company of this kind is a legal entity with power to make contracts in its own name but it seems that, in order to encourage the formation of such companies, the official view was that for income tax purposes such companies were to be regarded as the sums of the members; that is to say, that the income tax paid on dividends was to be regarded as tax paid by the individual shareholder while the company itself only paid tax on any profit which was retained.

There are two schools of thought about the distribution of profits. In this country it has always been thought virtuous on the part of the directors to distribute a comparatively small proportion of the available profit and to use the balance to build up the business to the long-term benefit of the shareholders by buying more modern machinery, building new factories, or opening new shops. The Government has in the past subscribed to this view by dividend limitation or by charging profits tax at a higher rate on distribution. Now, by the corporation tax, they have not only supported this view but have gone a step further by divorcing the shareholder from the company of which he is a member.

In some European countries the opposite view is held, and extra taxes are imposed on profits retained in the business as opposed to those distributed as dividends; the basic idea seems to be that the profits belong to the shareholders and should be distributed to them. The argument is that paying a higher dividend raises the price of the shares, thus making it easier for the company to raise fresh capital on advantageous terms. If the shareholder wishes to increase his stake in the company he can use part or all of his dividend to buy new shares; it is not right to compel him to do so by ploughing a substantial part of the profit back into the business instead of paying it out in dividend.

It has long been a basic principle of taxation in this country that the same income should not be taxed more than once. Profits tax infringed this rule since the amount levied on the company's income could not be credited against the shareholders' tax liability.

At the current rate of corporation tax, 45 per cent, and with income tax at 41·25 per cent, £100 of the original trading profit becomes £55 after £45 corporation tax and £32·31 after £22·69 income tax; the Inland Revenue has thus received £67·69 in tax. This compares with £56·25 which would have been taken by profits tax 15 per cent and income tax 41¼ per cent on £100 profit. Thus, £100 trading profit now only suffices to pay £32·31 net dividend; under the earlier tax system it would have sufficed to pay £43·75 net dividend.

There is another side to the picture: in the case of a company distributing less than one third the available profit, after 56¼ per cent profits tax and income tax, £100 profit would leave £43·75 available for distribution—say, £15 net dividend and £28·75 to increase the carry forward.

After 45 per cent corporation tax the £100 profit would leave £55 (gross) available for distribution, say, £15 (net) to the shareholder and £30 to increase the carry forward.

The immediate total tax comes to £55, of which £45 (corporation tax) is paid by the company; a net dividend of £15 costs the company £25; £15 (in round figures) to the shareholder and £10 income tax at 41¼ per cent payable to the Inland Revenue on behalf of the shareholder. This leaves £30 instead of £28·75 to increase the carry forward but it must be remembered that the extra £1·25 carried forward increases the total value of the company's capital and this must ultimately be reflected in a higher price for the shares, and that the shareholder—or his estate when he dies—will eventually suffer capital gains tax on that increase.

A company which in the past distributed only a small proportion of available profits as dividend scores under the new tax system while a company which distributed up to the hilt will suffer.

Although a limited liability company has a corporate entity of its own one cannot deny that it consists ultimately of its members. Corporation tax is levied on the profits of all limited liability companies instead of income tax and profits tax. Dividends are payable out of what is left after corporation tax, i.e. out of taxed profits. Income tax is deducted at the standard rate at source and paid to the Inland Revenue; therefore, with one or two exceptions, e.g. if franked investment income exceeds dividends payable, income tax will no longer appear in a company's accounts except as a debit to the shareholders and a corresponding credit to the Inland Revenue.

Before the advent of corporation tax, companies operating abroad were allowed to set off the local tax paid by them in the countries where the profit was earned against their liability for income tax and profits tax here; that is to say, if the local tax was at a lower rate than the United Kingdom tax, they had to pay the difference here but, if the local rate was higher, no further United Kingdom tax was payable but this is no longer the case.

Close Companies

The "close company" is a creature of the Finance Act, 1965. The legislation on this subject replaces that on surtax direction as applied to private companies controlled by five or fewer shareholders but casts the net much wider.

A company is outside the rules governing close companies if not less than 35 per cent of the voting ordinary shares are held by the public and quoted on a recognized Stock Exchange;

there must also have been dealings in that 35 per cent on a Stock Exchange during the previous twelve months and that 35 per cent must not include any shares held directly or indirectly by directors or their "associates".

The definition of, and the rules governing, close companies are complicated but the gist of the matter is that a company is "close" if it is controlled by five or fewer "participators". The term "participators" includes shareholders, option holders and loan creditors (other than banks and trade creditors); furthermore, a "participator" and his "associates" are treated as one person. "Associates" include his or her spouse, parents, grandparents, children and grandchildren, brothers and sisters, and partners, but not brothers-in-law unless they are partners. The rules are designed to prevent a "participator" from drawing out profits in a non-taxable form, e.g. by way of a loan, or in a form liable to tax at a lower rate, e.g. as excessive director's remuneration; they are also designed to prevent a "participator" from avoiding income tax and surtax by piling up reserves instead of paying dividends. By contrast, corporation tax is designed to encourage companies to pile up reserves and to discourage them from paying dividends.

By piling up reserves the public company must in the long run increase the value of its equity and this must be reflected in the price of its ordinary shares; the same applies to the "close" company though the process will take longer as the company is obliged to distribute sixty per cent of the net profits to shareholders by way of dividend.

DOUBLE TAXATION RELIEF

Bilateral double taxation relief agreements are in force between the United Kingdom and a number of countries including Canada, South Africa, and the United States.

"Non-resident" or "withholding" taxes are deducted from dividends paid by companies incorporated in the countries concerned from dividends paid to residents in the United Kingdom; these taxes are credited by the Inland Revenue against the income tax liability of the recipient.

The withholding tax is deducted from the gross amount of the dividend and U.K. tax at standard rate, minus withholding tax rate, is also deducted from the gross amount. The withholding tax rate in South Africa and the United States is 15 per cent and United Kingdom tax is deducted at 26¼ per cent on dividends from these countries.

In Canada, if the majority of the companies shares are held in that country, the rate is 10 per cent while, if the majority of the shares are held outside Canada, the rate is 15 per cent. United Kingdom shareholders suffer U.K. tax at 31¼ per cent in the former case and at 26¼ per cent in the latter.

Similarly, under the terms of the agreement, a resident in the United States receives dividends from companies incorporated in the U.K. with the deduction of U.K. withholding tax at 15 per cent instead of income tax at 41¼ per cent.

CHAPTER XII

Money Stocks and Investment Policy

WHEN business is good the tendency is for firms to enlarge their factories and increase their stocks and many of them borrow money to do this; if a firm believes that it can earn 15 or 20 per cent per annum, it is willing to pay 8 per cent, 9 per cent or even higher rates of interest on borrowed money, and interest rates rise since there are plenty of would-be borrowers.

When business is bad there is a dearth of borrowers as nobody wishes to pay rates of interest higher than, or even nearly as high as, the rate of profit which they expect to make on the loan; consequently it becomes almost impossible to lend money on good security, except at very low rates of interest. The bank rate is a fairly good indication of the rate at which money can be borrowed. A low rate stimulates borrowing and eventually stimulates business; as business improves more borrowers appear and interest rates gradually rise until they reach levels at which they definitely check business; and so it goes on in a series of trade cycles.

Those stocks which are backed by such good security that there is no doubt about the interest being paid at the due dates, such as British Government stocks and, to a lesser degree, well-secured industrial debentures, are known as money stocks.

The yield obtainable on these varies directly with the rate of interest at which money can be lent on good security. When money is more or less unlendable (on good security) the possessors of money buy "money stocks," since these offer a higher return on the money than can be obtained by lending it in the money market; the price of the money stocks consequently rises and the yield obtainable on them falls.

Money stocks can be divided into two classes; those with definite redemption dates which are not far distant and those which can only be redeemed many years hence or are irredeemable (or perpetual).

The former class, short-dated stocks, cannot rise in price very much above their par value, as the loss on redemption decreases the yield very considerably when the price rises much above par; similarly, even when money rates are high and the owners of these stocks sell them in order to employ the money to better advantage in the money market, the price does not fall much below par, since the profit obtainable on redemption increases the yield very considerably when the price falls, and thus attracts fresh buyers.

It is evident therefore that when money rates are low it is a wise policy to buy fairly short-dated securities (redeemable in, say, one to ten years' time) because, even if money rates rise, these are not likely to fall very much, particularly if a stock is chosen which can be bought below or only a little above the redemption price.

When money rates are high, it is wise to buy long-dated or perpetual stocks, as these will have fallen much more in proportion than the short-dated stocks, and offer a correspondingly larger scope for capital appreciation.

As a corollary to this, it is evident that when money rates are low the long-dated stocks, bought when the bank rate was high, should be sold and the proceeds invested in short-dated securities, or if no suitable stocks are available except at prices well above par, the money should be placed on deposit. When

Prices at which stock yields	10%	9%	8%	7%	6%	5%
3% stock	30	33 5/16	37 1/2	42 7/8	50	60
4% ,,	40	44 7/16	50	57 1/8	66 11/16	80
4½ ,,	45	50	56 1/4	64 1/4	75	90
5% ,,	50	55 9/16	62 1/2	71 1/2	83 5/16	100
5½% ,,	55	61 1/8	68 3/4	78 9/16	91 11/16	110
6% ,,	60	66 11/16	75	85 3/4	100	120
6½% ,,	65	72 3/16	81 1/4	93 1/16	108 5/16	130
7% ,,	70	77 3/4	87 1/2	100	116 5/8	140
7½% ,,	75	83 5/16	93 3/4	107 1/16	125	150
8% ,,	80	88 7/8	100	114 5/16	133 5/16	160
9% ,,	90	100	112 1/2	128 1/4	150	180
10% ,,	100	111	125	142 7/8	166 5/8	200

interest rates rise again, as they are bound to do eventually, the short-dated stocks can be exchanged for long-dated securities again.

Capital profits obtained in this way used to be free of tax except to banks, discount houses, and finance houses; now individuals and limited companies alike are assessable to capital gains tax though they can set off losses against profits.

Because of the nature of their business the discount houses invest mainly in short-dated British Government loans. British Government and British Municipal stocks with five years or less to final redemption date are known as "shorts" and are dealt in plus or minus so many days' interest calculated at the appropriate rate, i.e. so many days at 5 per cent per annum on a 5 per cent stock, 3 per cent per annum on a 3 per cent stock.

The interest is calculated in days reckoned from the last interest payment date to the next business day after the day of the bargain (i.e. the date when the stock should be delivered and paid for) and is added to the consideration. If the stock is dealt in after it has been made "ex dividend" but before the next interest payment date, interest for the number of days to the next interest payment date is subtracted.

The accrued interest is not regarded by the Inland Revenue as income but as an adjustment to the price. The seller who sold "ex dividend" or the buyer who bought "cum dividend" receives the actual interest payment and has to include it in his tax return. Shorts are said to be "clean" when dealt in minus so many days or plus only a few days.

As British Government stocks with less than five years to maturity rank as "liquid assets" when held by a clearing bank for the purpose of the liquid assets to deposits ratio, there is always a bigger demand from banks and discount houses for shorts than there is for medium- and long-dated British Government loans; although the discount houses are usually more interested in the very short-dated stocks, it is noticeable that there is often a marked rise in the price of a British Government loan on the day when it enters on its last five years and, technically, becomes a "short".

Unfortunately, the value of money is no longer stable and, although fixed-interest bearing securities may return to favour, it is probably no longer possible to float a loan without a final redemption date. The business cycle, too, is much less in evidence than it was before the last war and seems to have been replaced by a series of currency crises and fears of further devaluation of the pound. The result is that a great deal of money that would formerly have gone into fixed-interest bearing securities has been diverted into equities; it will be interesting to see whether falling profit margins, resulting at best in the same profit on a bigger turnover or in lower profits, or at worst in losses, will turn the tide back into fixed interest or whether fears of inflation will merely make investors more careful about choosing equity shares.

CHAPTER XIII

Investments

IN the good old days people spoke of the "absolute security" of certain investments, but nowadays we know that there is no such thing as absolute security, since even British Government securities—still probably the safest of all investments—gave their holders a nasty fright first in 1931 when Great Britain went off the gold standard and again in 1939 when minimum prices, below which no transactions were allowed, had to be introduced to support the market.

RELATIVE MERITS OF DIFFERENT TYPES OF INVESTMENT

British Government stocks, still termed "gilt-edged" though a good deal of the gilt has been rubbed off the gingerbread, rank as the soundest of holdings from the point of view that they are backed by the whole of the United Kingdom's resources and that you can be sure of the interest being paid on the due dates and that in the case of the dated stocks the capital will be repaid on the due date. Unfortunately nobody now knows what you will be able to buy with a pound sterling in twenty or even in ten years' time, and the heavy fall that has taken place in the prices of gilt-edged stocks and the high yields now obtainable on them are direct results of this uncertainty. Continual inflation, which the Government appears to be powerless to prevent, has produced the Trustee Investments Act, 1961, and this has no doubt contributed to the weakness of the gilt-edged market. Falling profit margins are now beginning to discourage investors from buying equities, and fixed-interest bearing securities may come into favour again, at any rate for the short term. Those who do not wish to invest in Government or Municipal stocks but require fixed-interest securities must turn their attention to debentures of sound industrial companies, water supply preference, or guaranteed stocks.

DEBENTURES

There are various points to examine when making the selection, but opinion has changed during recent years as to which points are of real importance.

The older text-books stress the advantage of mortgage debentures secured on certain definite assets and having the right of foreclosure should the interest not be paid.

More recently events have shown that, when a company gets into difficulties, it is quite the usual thing to propose a reconstruction involving sacrifices, not only from the shareholders (the proprietors), but from the debenture-holders (the creditors of the company) as well. A metaphorical pistol is levelled at the debenture-holders' heads and they are told that if they insist on their rights the company will be wound up, its assets sold for what they will fetch (i.e. next to nothing) and that after paying the expenses of liquidation there will be literally nothing left for them (the debenture-holders); whereas, if they will agree to a modification of their rights (e.g. accept a reduced rate of interest on their debentures, or possibly forgo the interest altogether unless it can be paid out of profits, and accept a certain number of ordinary shares per £100 of debenture stock held, as compensation for this sacrifice) it may be possible to save something for them out of the wreck. The debenture-holders usually protest but finally agree to make fairly substantial sacrifices, even though they are not quite as drastic as those originally suggested.

Modern opinion is less concerned with the specific security but tends to examine the cover, the provision made for redemption and the record of the company's financial policy. Questions such as the following are asked: "How much money is required to pay the annual debenture interest and how much was available during each of the last three or four years?" (i.e. what was the net pre-tax profit after providing for depreciation, but before paying the debenture interest). "How much of the net profit (after tax, depreciation and debenture interest) was distributed in dividends and how much put back into the business by way of reserve?"

If the profits of the business are not subject to wide fluctuations from year to year, and if the debenture interest is covered something like ten times and only about half of the net profit is distributed in dividends, the debenture looks pretty well "cast iron"; if, on the other hand, the debenture interest is only covered about one and a half times, and the net profit is distributed in dividend "up to the hilt," the debenture looks rather risky.

Another point to examine is whether the debenture is perpetual (irredeemable), redeemable only at the option of the borrower (the company), or whether it has a definite redemption date. Most of the debentures issued during the last ten years or so have to be redeemed by the company by a specified date and the company is usually obliged by the terms of the loan to pay a certain amount (e.g. $1\frac{1}{2}$ per cent of the nominal amount of the debentures still outstanding, or a fixed sum equal to 1 per cent or 2 per cent of the amount of the debentures originally issued) annually to a "sinking fund" before paying any dividends.

The sinking fund is used according to the terms of the issue of the debentures; it may be invested in gilt-edged securities, the interest from which is added to it every year, payments to the sinking fund being calculated to provide the money required to pay off the debentures at the redemption date. In other cases it may be used each year to buy debentures for cancellation, in the open market if they can be obtained at par (100 per cent) plus accrued interest or lower, or else to pay off debentures at par (or at a premium fixed by the terms of the issue), the debentures to be so paid off being selected by drawing lots.

A debenture whose interest requirements are well covered and which has a strong sinking fund as well, is a fairly safe investment, since you know that your money must be repaid in full by the final redemption date at the latest, and if that date is not too far distant—say, ten to thirty years—the sinking fund and the fact that the debenture must be redeemed on or before a certain date are very strong factors in maintaining the price.

A perpetual (or irredeemable) debenture, or one that is only redeemable at the company's (i.e. the borrower's) option, is not such a safe investment, since, should the company begin to make smaller profits, thus reducing the cover on the debenture interest, some of the debenture-holders would sell their stock and the price would fall in the absence of a sinking fund to support it.

As corporation tax is levied on profits after deduction of debenture and loan interest while preference dividends have to be paid gross (from the point of view of the company) out of profits remaining after corporation tax, it is cheaper to raise money by the issue of debentures or loans than to issue preference shares. The disadvantage is that the holder of debenture or loan stock is the creditor of the company whereas the holder of preference shares is not.

PREFERENCE SHARES

Preference shareholders rank for dividend after the interest has been paid to the debenture-holders, but before anything is paid to the ordinary shareholders. The holders of preference shares are part-proprietors of the company and dividends can only be paid to them out of profits; if the dividend is non-cumulative, then, if it is passed (when a dividend is not paid it is said to be "passed") in any one year because the company has not sufficient funds to make it prudent to pay it, the preference shareholders have no claim to any dividend for that year; if, however, the shares are entitled to a cumulative dividend all arrears of preference dividend have to be paid before any dividend can be paid to the ordinary shareholders. (It is customary to speak of cumulative and non-cumulative preference shares; strictly speaking, it is the dividend, and not the share, which is cumulative.)

The preference shares of some of the larger companies, with no debentures ranking before them and a large amount of dividend-paying ordinary capital behind them, e.g. Rowntree-Mackintosh, make a safer investment than the debentures of many smaller companies; the market opinion of the safety or otherwise of a security can be gauged by the yield obtainable at the current price—the higher the yield, the greater the risk. In the case of an ordinary share a low yield does not necessarily imply safety, but may be due to the market "discounting" the somewhat speculative possibilities of the share in question.

A comparatively recent innovation is the redeemable preference share, which possesses some of the characteristics of both
debentures and preference shares; the dividends are only payable out of profits, and such shares, therefore, provide less
security than debentures but may accordingly be expected to
give a better yield. On the other hand, they provide more
security in respect of capital since there is normally a definite
redemption date and the shares can usually be redeemed at a
premium at an earlier date at the option of the company. The
redemption terms should be studied carefully since it is clearly
inadvisable to buy shares at a price above that at which they
can be redeemed within a comparatively short time.

The "cover" for the dividend should be examined before
deciding to buy shares.

As preference shares rank after debentures and are therefore
less secure, one would expect to see them yielding more than
comparable debentures. This used to be the case but the advent
of corporation tax upset the apple-cart. One effect of this tax
is that debenture interest (being a charge to creditors) ranks
before corporation tax, whereas preference dividends (being a
distribution of profits to shareholders) rank afterwards. This
makes it more expensive for a company to service its preference
capital. A shareholder of a 5 per cent preference share receives
5 per cent gross, but it costs the company 10 per cent to pay
this. It would only cost the company 5 per cent to pay the
interest on a 5 per cent debenture.

As preference dividends are "franked" (i.e. they have suffered
corporation tax) they are sought by companies, as such income
is not liable to this tax a second time. This has led to a shortage
of preference shares which has been aggravated by the growing
practice of substituting debentures or loan stocks for preference
capital. For these reasons the yields on first class preference
shares have fallen below those on comparable debentures.

ORDINARY SHARES

When considering an ordinary share as an investment, after
calculating the yield on the assumption that the current rate of
dividend is maintained, it is instructive to calculate the yield on
earnings.

Consider two companies with the same capital consisting entirely of ordinary shares of £1, and engaged in a similar line of business; the shares of both companies can be bought at £2. "A" earned 12½ per cent on its capital and paid 12 per cent. (Dividend yield 6 per cent; earnings yield 6¼ per cent.) "B" earned 18 per cent on its capital but only paid 10 per cent in dividend. (Dividend yield 5 per cent; earnings yield 9 per cent.)

Which is the more attractive investment? The assumptions as to earnings, dividends and prices have been made as reasonable as possible, but they are, of course, entirely hypothetical.

The shares of "B" appear far more attractive (so much so, that it is unlikely that both shares would stand at the same price; it can be assumed, however, that a large block of the shares of "B" has come on to the market owing to the liquidation of a deceased account).

"A's" profits are being distributed up to the hilt and in the event of a bad year a reduction in the dividend would be necessary. "B's" profits leave a large margin over dividend requirements so that, although the directors might consider it advisable to reduce the dividend after a bad year, a very small cut might satisfy the claims of prudence. Also it must be remembered that the undistributed profit is not lost to the shareholder; on the contrary, it goes to strengthen the position of the company, either by being spent on replacing obsolete machinery with up-to-date plant, or by providing extra working capital, or by being invested in gilt-edged securities which can be turned into cash at short notice should the company require money at any time, and which bring in interest in the meanwhile. In any case, the shareholder reaps the benefit, since the undistributed profits add to the company's earning capacity; it is by "ploughing" a large part of the profits back into the business in this way that the prosperity of the large successful concerns has been built up.

When, after ten or twenty years, the earnings are so great that they permit the distribution of dividends of indecently large proportions (at least some people consider them indecent) part of the reserve equal, say, to the ordinary capital, is capitalized and new ordinary shares are issued as a bonus, free of charge, to the shareholders in the appropriate proportion (in this case one

new share for each old share held); if the capital bonus is 100
per cent (as just described) the rate of dividend is halved the
next year and looks less indecent, although the shareholders
receive exactly the same amount of cash. (Incidentally the price
of the shares would also be halved in this case.)

Two shining examples of this policy of conservative finance
are Courtaulds and Woolworths; here is an extract from the
chairman's speech at one of the annual general meetings of the
latter company: "The earnings on the ordinary share capital,
after providing, on the basis of a full year, interest on the
preferred shares, is 104·3 per cent, and the dividend for the
year is equal to 70 per cent. It may be thought by some that the
amount carried forward is too heavy, but your directors are
following the customary procedure of the company in building
up ample reserves. In this connection it is interesting to note
that this company has been brought from small beginnings to
its present robust condition through this policy of putting back
into the business a substantial proportion of the profits made, and
it will explain why the company has never since its inception
borrowed money or issued debentures. These profits are retained
in the business for the purpose of expansion, thus helping to
provide further profits for the shareholders."

If you have enough money to be able to spread your risk to
some extent it is worth while considering the ordinary shares of
companies with a good record since there is always the prospect
of gradually increasing dividends; there is of course the risk of
reduced dividends in bad years, but well-managed companies
distribute only a part of their net earnings while the balance is
put back into the business to increase its earning power, and
many companies now put an extra bit aside in good years to a
dividend equalization reserve to help to maintain the dividend
in lean times. The debenture and preference shareholders only
gain indirectly in that, as the cover for their interest or dividends
increases, the value of their securities tends to increase, too, but
sooner or later the ordinary shareholders will reap a real benefit
in the form of larger dividends.

It is worth remembering, too, that although the price of an
ox or a sheep averaged over a number of years tends to remain
constant in terms of the average day's wages of an unskilled
labourer, the cost of living in terms of money tends to rise from

decade to decade; thus the purchasing power of the income from a fixed-interest bearing investment gradually decreases as the years go by. This alone is a sufficient reason for putting at any rate a part of your savings into ordinary shares which give you a chance of maintaining the purchasing power of your income.

It is probably the fear of inflation which has driven money into such shares and has raised their prices to levels where the yields obtainable are often lower than can be obtained from an investment in gilt-edged stocks.

DEFAULT OF FOREIGN BONDS

Forty or fifty years ago only the very wealthy felt that they could afford to accept the low yields obtainable on British Government securities, industrial shares were not yet taken seriously and the chief field for investment by the middle classes was in foreign bonds.

Some countries have honoured their debts and have continued to do so; others honoured them so far as they were able, but the number of countries and states which have defaulted in bad times, but have taken no steps to resume payment in full when their circumstances improved, is depressingly large.

It has been said that foreign borrowers only made efforts to pay in order to keep their credit high in order to be able to borrow further sums on favourable terms; this is a sweeping statement but there is certainly an element of truth in it and, since the effect of the 1939–45 war is likely to make it impossible for this country to lend money abroad on any appreciable scale for years to come, that particular factor as an inducement to foreign countries to meet the interest and capital payments on their loans must be counted out for the present.

There is reason to believe that some foreign countries, while pleading their inability to find the money with which to pay the interest on their bonds which consequently fell in price, yet managed to find funds with which to buy their depreciated bonds for cancellation.

The Council of Foreign Bondholders have rendered yeoman service in looking after the interests of investors in foreign bonds but all the same it seems that this is a field that might well be left to the experienced investor.

"TAILORING" INVESTMENTS

The investment policy of trustees and of individuals must be tailored to fit individual requirements and this makes it most important that you should give your stockbroker as much information as possible. In the first place, if you have attained man's allotted span of three score years and ten, it is wise to have a proportion of your capital in Victory 4% (registered) Bonds since, if these have been held continuously for not less than six months before the date of death, the executors can tender them at 100 in payment of estate duty although they are only valued at the current market price for probate. At the time of writing the price is about 93½. Drawings take place in June every year and the bonds drawn are paid off at 100 on the following 1st September. The whole of the remaining bonds are expected to be paid off by 1976.

Now consider a younger man earning a good salary but due to retire in 1980; he does not need income now but when his salary is replaced by a pension he will want more from his investments. He would put part of his money into Treasury 3½ per cent stock 1977/80; at the present price of 63¼ the flat yield is £5·57 per cent, but every £63·75 invested now (63¼ + ½ commission) will become £100 free of capital gains tax by 15th June, 1980, when he can re-invest in something quite different. The capital profit is 36¼ points, a profit of 57 per cent in 10½ years. The redemption yield is 9·13 per cent gross and the net redemption yield with income tax at 41¼ per cent is 6·98 per cent.

Now, consider a still younger man whose children will have finished the most expensive part of their education by 1979 or 1980; he would want as much income as possible in the meantime and would put part of his money into, say, Funding 5¼ per cent 1978/80 at 74⅜ to yield 7¼ per cent flat and 6½ per cent to redemption. He might even go for a greater yield, say from a Corporation Stock such as Newcastle 9¼ per cent 1978/80, to yield 9⅝ per cent flat and 9⅞ per cent to redemption.

In view of inflation all these three might put some of their money into ordinary shares and there is a great deal to be said in favour of this course. The general feeling is that the lower the yield obtainable on a share, the greater the prospects of capital growth, and there is much to be said for this. It must not be forgotten, however, that the investor depends for his spending money, not on what the company in which he has invested earns, but on what it distributes in dividend. Where the price gives a tiny yield on current dividends it seems to be giving a hostage to fortune to buy the shares on the basis of the trebled or quadrupled dividend that you expect the company to pay four or five years hence. An alternative view is that small sales of such growth shares can be made annually to supplement the small income and therefore treat part of the capital as income. This is all very well when prices are rising but in a falling market the value of an investment will be eroded still further by this action.

Cancer scares cause a fall in the prices of tobacco companies from time to time but the consumption of tobacco seems to go on increasing and the Government derives such an enormous proportion of the national revenue from tobacco duty that little action seriously to reduce smoking is likely. Tobacco companies give a good yield and some are taking steps to diversify their interests in fields other than those of tobacco. Imperial Tobacco for instance launched Golden Wonder Crisps and have taken over H P Sauce. Their mammoth investment portfolio must not be forgotten.

The insurance companies probably give as good scope for capital growth as any; owing to inflation a man who would formerly have insured his life for £500 now insures it for £1,000 and he probably doubles his fire insurance on his house as well; however, the yields on insurance shares and on bank shares are comparatively low and if you buy these you must be prepared to be patient, ignore price fluctuations and wait for your dividends to be increased. However, companies which write American business have had some unfortunate experiences. Competition has kept rates down while repair bills and damages have become more expensive, while the toll of hurricanes appears to have increased.

THE SMALL INVESTOR

It is of the greatest importance that everybody, and particularly the small investor, should realize that the prices of even the soundest securities fluctuate considerably from time to time. The investor must be able to ignore these fluctuations; in practice this means that he must keep a sum of money in his current account or on deposit in the Post Office Savings Bank or in a Building Society to meet any emergency, so that he can sell his shares when he wants to do so because the price is high, and not be forced to sell them when the price is low for want of ready cash. Emergencies involving a need for cash usually occur at times when prices are low. The small investor would be well advised to put his savings into the Post Office Savings Bank or a Building Society until he has built up a capital of £500 or £600 and then take out about £400 for his first Stock Exchange investment.

In America stockbrokers woo the small investor since on small transactions their commissions are as high as 6 per cent in addition to transfer expenses, which are low. In this country most stockbrokers will carry out small transactions as a matter of public duty but, as the commission on an investment of £100 in Government stock may be as low as one per cent, they do not seek out this kind of business, which brings them no profit.

It is impossible to calculate the cost of a bargain but some idea can be obtained by dividing the year's expenses (rent, salaries, stationery, postage, telephones, etc.) by the number of bargains done, and on this basis no bargain is likely to cost under £4.

When you decide to carry out your first Stock Exchange transaction you will doubtless find a friend who can recommend a stockbroker to you and give you an introduction but, if not, you should write to the Secretary to the Council, The Stock Exchange, London, E.C.2; you will be sent a list of some twenty firms who have intimated their willingness to undertake business introduced in this way; you should then write to the firm you select, mentioning that their name has been submitted to you by the Stock Exchange authorities and giving references (preferably a bank). The list sent to prospective clients is worked on a rota and is changed every month to distribute the business fairly.

When you approach a stockbroker for the first time to ask for advice about investments, it is a good thing to give him some idea of your general circumstances and of what if any, investments you already hold, since he is bound to take these into consideration before he can offer an opinion.

A share with speculative possibilities may be a reasonable purchase for a bachelor earning £2,000 a year and with several thousand pounds already invested in British Government loans and first-class equity shares, yet a purchase of shares in the same company by a £1,000 a year married man with a couple of children and no invested capital could only be regarded as foolhardy speculation.

If a wealthy client wishes to invest a considerable sum of money, his broker finds it relatively easy to make a list of suggestions which will spread the risk over various industries dealing with home and foreign markets and ranging from banks and insurance companies to ship-building, from breweries and tobacco firms to mining companies and from agricultural machinery makers to multiple stores, giving brief notes of his reasons for recommending them, knowing that his client has sufficient experience to enable him to make his own decisions on the information supplied.

When a client approaches him for advice about the invest-ment of a relatively small sum, he has a much harder task, since the money cannot be spread over more than two or three different securities without incurring disproportionately high expenses, and the importance of avoiding the risk of losses is relatively much greater.

A request for advice on the investment of a small sum entails more work for the broker, involves him in more worry since he knows that he will blame himself if in the end his client sustains a loss which the broker knows that he can ill afford, and brings him little profit, since the commissions charged on small orders do not even cover the overhead charges.

You need not be shy, however, in approaching a broker even if you have only a small amount to invest; most brokers wel-come such inquiries, remembering that the small client of today is often the big client of tomorrow when he has climbed to the top of his own profession or business or inherited a fortune from his rich uncle. "Little fish are sweet!"

Incidentally, no investment should be regarded as permanent and if your list of securities is too large to be carried in your head you should go through it carefully at least once or twice a year and consider whether some of the items could not with advantage be exchanged for something safer or more promising; this applies particularly to trustees since trust funds are apt to be invested in stocks which appear to be perfectly safe at the time and are then put away and forgotten; ten or twenty years later the trustees wake up and wish they had had an annual overhaul which might well have resulted in selling some of their securities before the fall in price had become really serious.

INVESTMENT TRUSTS

In order to enable the small investor to spread his risk Investment Trust Companies were formed to buy securities and distribute the investment income to their shareholders; some confined their attention to specific types of security, e.g. foreign Government bonds; others displayed more catholic tastes but all sought to reduce the risk by spreading their holdings over different parts of the world and over different kinds of enterprise; their shareholders benefited from having their investments managed by men whose training, experience and intimate contact with the market enabled them to take swift advantage of any favourable opportunity of selling one security and replacing it with another.

Formerly, there was only a narrow market in investment trust shares. In good times the shares were tightly held and it was almost impossible to buy them; in bad times it was equally difficult to find a buyer at anything like a reasonable price. Now, there is a much freer market, owing to many of the trusts having a much bigger issued capital as a result of capitalization issues, rights issues and mergers. There is usually little difficulty in selling shares and if one cannot buy shares in any particular trust it is easy to find shares in a similar investment trust to give a similar yield.

It may be useful to explain the difference between investment trusts and finance trusts. Investment trusts hold securities for income which they distribute by way of dividend and are careful not to sell any investment, unless they have obviously made a bad blunder in buying it, until it has paid one or two dividends since, if they make too frequent changes of investment, the Inland Revenue may insist on taxing them as finance trusts.

To obtain the advantages of ranking as an investment trust a company's articles of association must preclude the distribution of capital profits except in the form of capitalization issues and it must distribute not less than 85 per cent of its investment income as dividend. Except for the 1962 short-term capital gains tax, which hardly applied as investment trusts rarely sold securities within six months of buying them—they risked being taxed as finance trusts if they made a practice of doing so—their capital profits were exempt from tax. They are now liable,[1] irrespective of the time for which the securities have been held, not at corporation tax rate as in the case of other companies, including finance trusts, but at 30 per cent, the rate applicable to individual investors; so that investment trust shareholders should not be taxed twice over on what is fundamentally the same profit, investment trusts are obliged by law to issue capital gains tax vouchers similar to the income tax vouchers attached to dividend warrants. When the shareholder takes a profit on shares in an investment trust he can submit his capital gains tax voucher to the Inland Revenue to show how much tax has already been paid on his profit.

Corporation tax is levied on income received by a company in the form of debenture or loan interest, and on dividends from overseas companies, since these have not borne corporation tax (unfranked income). Companies are not liable for corporation tax on income received in the form of preference or ordinary dividends paid by United Kingdom companies which have already borne this tax (franked income).

Finance trusts set out to make profits by buying and selling securities; their capital profits as well as their other income were subject to income tax and profits tax and are now subject to corporation tax; their capital profits were and still are distributable as dividend in the same way as other income. Finance trusts could deduct capital losses from profits liable to tax, while investment trusts, which paid no tax on capital profits, had to bear their capital losses in full. Now finance trusts can still deduct capital losses from profits assessable to corporation tax but investment trusts can only set them off, or carry them forward to be set off, against capital profits.

It appears that between the wars the funds of some of the

[1] See footnote on p. 101.

investment trusts in the U.S.A. were used for gambling and even to buy unsuccessful speculations from the managers to such an extent as to bring the whole idea of a "managed investment trust" into disrepute in America; the Fixed Trust, which first appeared in England as long ago as 1868, emerged as the result and then returned to England in the nineteen-thirties. The Fixed Trust proved to be too rigid and has now developed into the Flexible Unit Trust.

UNIT TRUSTS

Although they are closely bound up with the Stock Exchange, only a few unit trusts are actually quoted on the Stock Exchange.

There are three parties to a unit trust, namely, the unit holders who have invested in them, the trustee, usually a bank or insurance company, which acts as custodian for the underlying securities, maintains a register of unit holders, issues unit certificates and pays the dividends, and the managers, who invite subscriptions, buy and sell units and the underlying securities, select the securities in which the funds of the unit holders may be invested, and are generally responsible for investment policy; the success of the unit trust depends mainly on the expertise of the managers.

In order to comply with the Prevention of Frauds Act, 1958, all unit trusts must conform to Board of Trade Regulations, which cover the method of calculating the price, management charges, etc. The prices at which the underlying securities can be bought or sold are ascertained at the opening of business in the Stock Exchange every morning; the total cost of buying the underlying securities plus transfer expenses plus Stock Exchange commission plus Settlement Duty ($\frac{1}{4}$ per cent of value of the Trust Fund) plus service charge (say, 5 per cent) is then calculated; this sum, divided by the number of units, gives the price of the unit which is then "rounded up" to the nearest multiple of 0·1 penny, and this is the price at which units can be bought from the managers on that day. (The price can be altered if there is a violent change in the price of one or more of the underlying securities during the day.)

Similarly, the price at which units can be sold to the management is calculated from the prices at which the underlying securities can be sold, less the commission, and rounded down to the nearest multiple of 0·1 penny (Board of Trade Regulations allow rounding up or down to the nearest multiple of 1¼p. or 1 per cent of the amount, whichever is the less.)

The leading unit trust management companies operate a number of different trusts, each aiming for specific objectives. The most common sort of unit trust, the "general" trust, aims at providing capital growth combined with a reasonable level of income. Other trusts, the "capital" trusts, aim at maximum capital growth by investing in growth shares with little yield; the "income" trusts are invested into higher yielding shares with less prospects of capital growth. There are "property" unit trusts, "bank and insurance" trusts, "commodity" trusts and even unit trusts investing solely in the shares of investment trusts, to mention but some.

These specialist trusts often have to be watched as closely as an equity: their performance depends very largely on that of their particular sector of the market.

Many trusts now have "accumulator units" which provide for the income being re-invested into the fund to provide greater capital growth.

Some of the daily newspapers publish tables comparing the performance of the different funds. While this is a useful guide, it must be remembered that the management of a trust can change hands making past performance meaningless. Also, the investor who bought a property unit trust after a year of rising property share prices which caused the fund to perform well above average, would find himself with a loss if that sector of the market then fell. Equally, it is human nature for managers to advertise those funds which have done well in recent times, whereas it is the funds that are depressed, such as the capital trusts at the end of a bear market, which should be bought.

These unit trusts are a splendid means for the very small investor to spread his risk widely and are very convenient for those who wish to invest small sums every month, but they do appear to be rather an expensive way of investing one's money. However, if you want to buy one cigarette at a time rather than buy a packet of ten or twenty you must expect to pay for the privilege.

In favour of unit trusts it should be noted that many of them are sponsored by firms of the highest financial reputation and that by 1969 it was estimated that about £1,384 million was invested in them, most of the money, presumably, having come from people who would not venture to invest in Stock Exchange securities in the ordinary way.

It is also interesting to note that, although the Stock Exchange is prepared to grant quotation to unit trusts subject to fairly stringent requirements, so far only a few unit trusts, all from the same stable, have applied for and obtained quotation; there must be many others which could obtain quotation but have not thought it worth while to do so. The advantage of quotation to the unit holder is that he can obtain a closer price in his units, i.e. a smaller margin between the prices at which he can sell his units or buy more.

Under the Finance Act 1972, investment trusts and unit trusts pay Capital Gains Tax at 15 per cent (instead of 30 per cent); unit-holders or shareholders who take profits on their holdings, if liable to Capital Gains Tax, will pay 15 per cent on such profits but will not be able to reclaim repayment of 15 per cent Capital Gains Tax if not liable. Capital Gains Tax vouchers will no longer be issued.

CHAPTER XIV

The Stock Exchange
and the Public Interest

THE Stock Exchange was formed originally as a profit-making concern but it has developed, particularly of recent years, into a powerful guardian of the interests of the general public; it imposes a strict code of rules on its members and has disciplinary powers which enable it to enforce them. These or similar rules govern the members of the provincial Stock Exchanges.

By dealing only through members of one of the recognized Stock Exchanges you obtain the protection of the Stock Exchange Council or of the provincial Stock Exchange authorities against any infringement of your rights.

Naturally this does not mean that the fact that the shares of a company are dealt in on the Stock Exchange guarantees that the company will prosper and that you will not lose money by buying its shares or even that there is a free market in the shares.

The Stock Exchange Council are, however, continually tightening up the requirements which must be satisfied by companies before permission is given to deal in their shares on the Stock Exchange.

These requirements have been framed in order to obtain for the shareholder the fullest possible information as to the financial position of his company and to assist him as far as may be in exercising his vote in its control. As an illustration it may be mentioned that companies seeking permission for their shares to be dealt in on the Stock Exchange are required to undertake to give full notice of their meetings and, if they send out proxies, to draw them up in such a way that the shareholder or debenture holder can vote either in favour of or against the resolution put forward. They must also undertake to publish, immediately after the board meeting, all dividends declared or recommended and at the same time to make known the net profits for the year with the figures for the previous year for comparison and any other information necessary to prevent the creation of a false impression which would lead to an unjustified rise or fall in the price of the shares.

OUTSIDE HOUSES

Earlier editions of this book contained warnings against dealing with "bucket shops" but these have virtually disappeared as the result of the Prevention of Fraud (Investment) Act under which it is illegal to deal in stocks and shares unless licensed by the Board of Trade or exempt by virtue of membership of a recognized Stock Exchange.

When dealing with a Stock Exchange firm you will get a contract note showing exactly what the shares have cost or realized and how much has been charged for commission so that you can see what you are paying your broker for his services.

When you deal with an "Outside House" you may deal at a net price which includes an unspecified amount of commission, or you may deal at a price which includes the commission paid by the "Outside House" plus commission (on a purchase) or less commission (on a sale) charged by the "Outside House." The Stock Exchange still refers to outside firms as "bucket shops" but many, probably most, of them are honest firms who prefer to remain independent of Stock Exchange rules and regulations in order to be free to advertise and to address their circulars to all and sundry.

When dealing in shares in which there is an active market these firms cannot hope to compete with the Stock Exchange but it is probably fair to say that a large part of their turnover is in the shares of sound but small businesses in which, on account of the small size of their capital, there can never be a really free market.

Many people have bought shares in this way and have had no cause to regret their action until, for some reason or other, they have wanted to turn their shares into cash without delay. Then they have found that the capital of the company was too small for anything like a free market to develop and that they were faced with the alternatives of waiting for weeks or months till a buyer appeared or of accepting a knock-out price in order to effect a quick sale, although the shares themselves were perfectly sound and paying good dividends.

Outside firms normally buy such shares as opportunity offers (through the Stock Exchange as often as not) and then peddle them around; there is, however, no guarantee that they will have capital available to lock up in shares of this kind just when you are anxious to sell your holding.

Their business is to buy and sell shares on their own account and they send out circulars offering the shares that they wish to sell and bidding for shares for which they know that they have buyers; it is no part of their business to draw the attention of possible purchasers to the poor marketability of the shares they are offering, though it is legitimate for them to stress their merits.

Outside firms usually claim in their circulars that the client can deal through them to better advantage than he can through the ordinary channels. A moment's reflection will show the absurdity of this claim; the outside firm cannot do better than buy the shares in the open market, i.e. the Stock Exchange. It thus pays the same price and commission that the client would have paid if he had dealt with a Stock Exchange firm; as the outside house does not do the business for love, it is evident that the client must pay more by dealing with an outside house. A similar argument may be used *mutatis mutandis* with regard to selling shares. The alternative is for the outside house to sell shares already in its possession and, as it will obviously not sell them at a lower price than that obtainable in the open market, the client will not be buying shares particularly cheaply.

Even if you only deal with a Stock Exchange firm there are plenty of pitfalls. In particular you must be on your guard against promiscuous tips. When business is brisk there are always plenty of tips going about to the effect that "it is right to buy" this or that share for a quick profit. Mr. Z believes that a director of a certain mining company has been buying shares in the company for himself and argues that the director probably has good reason for so doing; Mr. Z buys himself a thousand shares and tells all his pals, some of whom do likewise. By the time you hear of it the price has risen, these people start taking their profits and, if you buy the shares, you probably get "landed at the top." Mr. Y notices that the price of Consolidated Bottlewashers has fallen of late; inquiring the reason why, he learns that one of the largest shareholders has died recently and that his estate is being wound up. Further inquiry convinces him that the bulk of this holding has already been sold; as soon as "the tap has been turned off" the price should rise to its previous level, he thinks, so he "tips" Consolidated Bottle-washers for a rise; and so it goes on, tips to buy for a rise being far more frequent than tips to sell for a fall, owing to the innate optimism of the human race.

ODDS AGAINST THE SPECULATOR

You must remember that if you, an outsider, start speculating, as opposed to investing, the odds are fairly heavily against you. To begin with, by the time the tip reaches you, it is probably already too late; then, as you are not on the spot you cannot take advantage of a momentary rise to "get out"; and lastly, you have the jobber's turn and the broker's commission against you.

Consider a share standing at about £0·85. Suppose that there is a free market and that there is a 1p price; the commission is just under 1¼p. Your broker finds that the price is £0·84½–£0·85½, and you buy 200 shares at £0·85½; suppose that immediately afterwards, before the price has moved, you decide that it was a mistake to buy and you sell them again at once; you only get £0·84½ for them, so that you have lost 1p a share plus 1¼p per share commission, equals 2¼p per share.

If you buy and sell the same shares during the same "Account" your broker may, at his discretion, charge only one commission—either on the original bargain or on the closing bargain. For the sake of convenience, full commission is generally charged on the opening bargain and the second bargain is done "free to close." If the £5,000 rule concession[1] was made on the opening bargain, the closing bargain would entail charging the balance of the full commission because only one concession may be made on the same set of bargains.

To put it in another way, if you have bought shares at £0·85½ which enjoy a sufficiently free market for it to be possible to deal at a 1p price, you cannot get out without a loss, let alone make a profit, before the price has risen 2¼p. If the market is less active and the price consequently wider, the shares must rise

---

[1] The £5,000 rule is now embodied in the main scale and both concessions can, in effect be made.

further before you can get out without loss; e.g., if there is a
3p price and you "got in" at £0·85½ (price £0·82½–£0·85½),
the price must rise from £0·82½ bid to £0·85½ plus 1¼p (commission) equals £0·86¾ bid, before you can get out without loss
—a rise of 4¼p within one account. After that you must allow
for transfer stamp and a second commission as well.

Tips quite often "come off" but it is extremely difficult, if not
impossible, to distinguish between good and bad tips until after
the event. If you ignore all tips you will miss making some
handsome profits, but you will avoid even larger losses, unless
your broker is cautious and well-informed above the average—
and that you can only judge by watching the prices in the daily
papers and seeing what would have happened if you had
followed his advice.

It should be pointed out here that when you ask your broker
for advice his job is to prevent you from losing money rather
than to make money for you. The two things are by no means
the same. He may dissuade you from following a dubious tip
which turns out well, but you should not reproach him for that.
If, on the other hand, he encourages you to buy something
speculative without pointing out the risk, you have good
grounds for complaint if it turns out badly.

FUTURE PROSPECTS

The writer's view is that there is only one way for the small
investor to make money on the Stock Exchange, and that is a
very slow one. He must buy a good stock or share, taking care
not to buy it immediately after a sharp rise (for rises are often
followed by a reaction due to profit taking), to yield him a certain annual income and keep it ("sit on it") until he sees a
chance of exchanging it for another security of similar standing
which will yield the same income and give sufficient profit on
the transaction, after paying the expenses, to make it worth
while. Issues of new shares and debentures by old-established
companies are attractive since there are no transfer expenses to
pay; it can be more satisfactory to buy them in the market
than to apply for them direct. (*See* chapter on New Issues.)

In this connexion two classes of ordinary shares stand out as
particularly suitable for investment with an eye to eventual

capital appreciation. No one can foresee which industries are going to produce the great and prosperous companies of ten or twenty years hence—to take one example—who guessed, sixty years ago, that the manufacture of gramophones and records would one day become a huge and flourishing industry? It seems fairly certain however, that banks and discount companies will always be wanted to finance trade, whether the commodities are wheat and pig-iron or silk stockings and television apparatus, and insurance companies are not likely to become obsolete on account of increasing longevity and improved fire-engines; accidents always have happened and always will.

It must be remembered that when a company secures a very large contract which "hits the headlines" it does not necessarily follow that the company will make a correspondingly large profit; it may have had to cut profits to the bone, in order to secure the order in face of fierce competition, or it may even have deliberately accepted the contract at a loss to keep the works going and so avoid the dispersal of its skilled artisans; this has happened more than once in the shipbuilding industry.

Similarly, although the discovery of a new oil-field or ore-body often raises the price of the shares of the company concerned, it should not be forgotten that, before any profit from the discovery can materialize, the company will have to invest vast sums over a number of years to finance the sinking of oil wells or mine shafts and for the building of pipe-lines railways, roads and harbours.

CHAPTER XV

Stock Exchange Psychology

IF you decide to speculate you should try to learn something of Stock Exchange psychology; although the Stock Exchange is notoriously short-sighted, it is much more inclined to deal in what it believes is going to happen next week, or next year, than in what actually happened yesterday.

The result is that if good news is expected—i.e. the declaration of an increased dividend in good times, or of a maintained dividend in present circumstances—people buy the shares in anticipation, thus causing the price to rise; as soon as the news is out, there is "nothing more to go for" and they all hurry to take their profits; this brings the price down and gives the bargain-hunter his chance.

Conversely, if a bad report is expected the bears get busy and the price falls; as soon as the news appears, the bears rush to cover their commitments (i.e. buy back the shares which they have sold but do not possess) and the price recovers.

This explains the paradox of good news causing the price to fall while bad news is followed by a rise. Of course, if the news is entirely unexpected, it has the effect on the price that one would expect.

A great difficulty is to know when to sell. There are two well-known Stock Exchange sayings which are mutually contradictory—"Nobody ever went broke through taking a profit" to which one might add "provided he does nothing foolish with the proceeds" and "Cut a loss and run a profit."

If you have bought shares as a speculation, it is wise to heed the former saying, take a reasonable profit if you get the chance, and be thankful; if you have bought the shares as an investment, keep them as long as they continue to forge ahead, ignoring minor day-to-day fluctuations. It is worth pointing out that if after twelve months you can clear a profit of 10 per cent after allowing for dealing expenses, i.e. a net profit of 7 per cent with capital gains tax at 30 per cent, you have made nearly as much as you would have received by way of income in two and a half years, with income tax at the present rate of £0·41¼ per cent, if you had invested in a safe security yielding 5 per cent. Since short-term capital gains are taxed as income, if you can make a clear profit of 5 per cent in a few weeks you have made as much as you would have received in a full year by investing at a yield of 5 per cent. This is not meant to be an incitement to rash speculation; on the contrary, it is meant to make you realize that, if you have been skilful or fortunate enough to make such profits, you need not be in a hurry to re-invest the money but can regard it as having "earned its keep" for the balance of the two and a half years (or one year), and be content to let it lie idle in the bank for a bit until you see a really good chance of repeating the performance.[1]

An even more difficult decision to make is when to cut a loss; we are most of us optimists at heart and we all hate to admit having made a mistake, but if shares have been bought for a speculation and the price refuses to rise or, worse still, starts to go down, then, nine times out of ten it is wise to get out quickly.

Some investors, if the price falls after they have bought their shares and if they have confidence in their judgement, buy more on the fall to "average" and then, if the price recovers to its original level, sell the lot and heave a sigh of relief.

Other, probably shrewder, investors in similar circumstances hold their hand while the price is falling but, if it recovers, double their holding at the original price with the remark "I was right after all" and then go on to make a large profit.

The chief value of an investment is to provide you with an income and banish financial worries, so, if a particular holding causes sleepless nights, the only thing to do is to sell it, however good it may be, and buy something less disturbing.

While on this subject it may be as well to consider the case of a man who is bemoaning the fact that he bought 1,000 Patent Sausage Machine ordinary shares when they stood at £1·25 and that the present price is only £0·50; he complains that he cannot

---

[1] Short-term Capital Gains Tax has now been abolished.

afford to sell them now as he would be realizing a loss of over £0·75 a share. It is true, from one point of view, that it is only a loss on paper until the shares have been sold and the loss realized, but it is surely also true that his shares at this moment represent £500 cash—what he paid for them is ancient history and quite irrelevant—and that unless he can honestly say to himself "If I had £500 cash I would invest it in 1,000 P.S.M. ordinary shares rather than in anything else" he would be well advised to sell his Patent Sausage Machine shares and invest the proceeds in something sounder.

It is a counsel of perfection to suggest a periodical overhaul of one's holdings followed by a sale of everything that has failed to fulfil the expectation on the strength of which it was bought, though such a course will often prevent larger losses later on. If you have to sell something the temptation is to take a profit but if this is done regularly the investor will find he has got rid of all his good holdings and kept the bad ones; sell the shares which have done the worst, is a general rule.

The shares in all sound companies have three zones of prices although it is virtually impossible to define their boundaries; below a certain level the shares are obviously cheap and should be bought; above a certain level the shares, however good the company, are over-valued and should be sold, and between those two levels there is a range where the shares are not cheap enough to be worth buying but are still worth keeping. Investment portfolios, like gardens, are improved by careful weeding as well as by pruning holdings which seem to be becoming too exuberant.

Many people find it difficult to understand how you can sell what you have not got; this comes from confusing two separate and distinct operations which, in ordinary life, are closely bound up together; when your tobacconist sells you a packet of cigarettes he first agrees to sell you the packet at the market price, he then delivers it by handing it to you and then accepts payment by picking up the cash that you have put on the counter; the whole thing is done practically in one movement.

When your gramophone dealer takes your order for a particular record that is not in stock, he does not sell a bear but merely undertakes to get it for you if he can.

In the Stock Exchange, when a bargain is done, the seller contracts to deliver the stock on or soon after a specified date against payment and the buyer contracts to pay for it against delivery; when a bear sells what he does not possess, he has until the end of the account in which to buy it or borrow it ("take-in") for delivery against his sale. Of course, if he buys it back from the person to whom he sold it, no stock changes hands but the difference in price between the two bargains is adjusted in cash unless both bargains were done at the same price.

CHAPTER XVI

Contangos: Carrying Over

WHEN a man has bought shares, the price of which he expects to rise, as a speculation and has not got the ready cash with which to pay for them, he can very often get his broker to "carry them over" for him. That is to say, he sells the shares for the old account, buys them at the same price for the new account and pays a "contango" or interest on the money involved. The price fixed is the middle price (i.e. halfway between the price at which the shares can be sold and the price at which they can be bought) at the close of the market on the final Thursday of the Account and contangos must be arranged on the final Friday. In an Account covering Easter, Christmas, or some other holiday, for "final Friday" read "final Wednesday" or "final Thursday," as appropriate. In a normal Account "final Thursday" is a more convenient expression than the "penultimate day of the Account."

The broker may charge a commission for carrying over but usually his remuneration is included in the rate of interest, i.e. he charges his client ½ per cent or 1 per cent per annum higher interest than he pays in the market. The client in this case is said to be a "bull" of the shares. A bull is always an optimist, at any rate as far as the prospects of the shares of which he is a bull are concerned, since he thinks that the price is going to rise; "bullish" consequently is the Stock Exchange slang for optimistic.

If the price has fallen since he bought the shares, the client is expected to pay the difference between the price at which he bought them and the contango (or "making up") price on account day to square his account; if the price has risen his broker pays him the difference. The broker, however, unless he knows his client very well and is assured of his financial standing, will expect him to keep a credit balance or deposit a certain amount of securities (bearer for choice) with him to cover a possible loss in case the price of the shares falls heavily. If the price falls and this cover or margin runs off, the broker will demand further cover and if this is not forthcoming, he is entitled to sell the shares in order to cut the loss. The client is, of course, liable for the whole of the loss incurred.

It is often convenient to carry shares over for one or two accounts in order to save transfer stamp and fee, but it should be remembered that the stamp and fee only amount to about 1 per cent of the consideration (i.e. the money paid for the shares apart from commission, etc.); the contango rate on a speculative share is usually 8 per cent or 9 per cent per annum. The length of an account is a fortnight or roughly $\frac{1}{24}$ of a year, so that if the rate is 8 per cent per annum, you pay approximately $\frac{1}{3}$ per cent per account; in other words, if you pay 8 per cent contango for four accounts, you have spent as much in interest as you would have done in paying for the stamp and fee. If you have the money lying idle or on deposit at the bank, it is cheaper to "take up" the shares unless you only intend to "run them" for an account or two.

A bull, even if he has carried the shares over, is entitled to any dividends or rights declared on the shares after he has bought them and before he has sold them again.

If a man thinks that the price of a share is likely to fall, he sells them, even if he does not possess any, and he is then said to be a "bear" of the shares, or to be "short" of them. When the end of the account comes, if he cannot deliver the shares (since he has none to deliver) or does not wish to deliver them, since they are registered in his name and he hopes to buy them back at a lower price, and does not wish to have to pay another stamp and fee, he instructs his broker to "take them in" (or "borrow" them).

If there are plenty of "bulls" about, the broker arranges the carry-over as described above, except that in this case the client receives interest instead of paying it. The broker either charges him a commission for carrying over or, more usually, pays him a $\frac{1}{2}$ or 1 per cent lower rate of interest per annum than he receives in the market. Leeman's Act, passed in 1867, prohibited all dealings in Bank shares except by real holders. It was, therefore, illegal to sell a bear of Bank shares and neither options nor contangos were allowed. However, this act was repealed in

1967 but escaped the notice of the option dealers until 1969 and bank option deals were then resumed.

When a "bear" takes shares in he buys them for the old account and sells them at the same price for the new account; the price is fixed in the same way as for the bull. If the price has risen since he sold the shares the bear has to pay the difference to square his account while, if it has fallen, he receives the difference. The broker will expect his client to keep a credit balance with him or to deposit securities as cover against a possible loss, whether he is a bull or a bear.

Theoretically, when stock or shares are carried over, the bull lends stock to the bear and the bear lends money to the bull.

As money can always be borrowed if the rate of interest offered is high enough, a bull can always "get on" at a price— if the worst comes to the worst the broker "takes up" the shares for him and charges him stamp and fee as well as interest on the money—but, if there are more bears than bulls, the bears may have to take in the shares at "evens" (i.e. without receiving any interest on the money) or, if there is a large number of bears, they may have to borrow the shares and pay a backwardation or "back" on them. (A "back" is the opposite of a contango: a contango is the rate paid by a bull on the money which he borrows with which to pay for the shares and which is lent to him by the bear who is "taking the shares in"; a "back" is the payment which is made by a bear on the shares which he borrows to deliver against his sale.)

Certain jobbers keep a "book" in contangos and brokers who have contango business indicate their requirements to the jobber shortly before the end of the account. When dealings for the account stop at 5.00 p.m. on the last day, the jobber matches "bulls" and "bears" where possible but any broker whose position cannot be matched may be unable to do his contango and would then be obliged to close his position for "cash" free to close before 6.30 p.m.

A bull's maximum loss is limited to the amount he paid for the shares, since the price cannot fall below nothing (unless there is a liability attached to the shares—partly paid shares or shares in a company with unlimited liability) while his possible profit is, theoretically, unlimited; a bear's maximum profit is the amount for which he sold the shares (if they become valueless he can buy them back for nothing) but his possible loss is unlimited.

A man who sells shares which he possesses but does not wish to deliver is said to be a "protected bear."

A bear must hand over to the buyer any dividends or rights declared on the shares after he has sold them; if he is a protected bear with the shares registered in his name, the dividends will be paid to him but they do not belong to him for all that.

Bears exert a steadying influence on markets since they sell on a rapid rise and thus check it, while, when the price falls suddenly, they buy back their shares and thus support the market. A large bear account is a source of strength to the market, while a large bull account is a source of weakness.

When a broker carries shares over (whether it is for a bull or a bear) he issues a "continuation" contract to show what he has done.

Many years ago there was a very big business in contangos and large speculative positions were "continued" for long periods. As far as can be judged this kind of business has shrunk to a mere trickle and many stockbroking firms refuse to do any contango business at all.

CHAPTER XVII

Options

FIRST, we may consider what is meant by an "option". The word option means a choice; the choice of whether or not to deal in shares at a future date at today's price. A sum of money, called option money, must be paid for this privilege. Options may be done on the Stock Exchange for any period not exceeding three months. The majority of options are done for the maximum period, but they may be exercised during any account until they expire.

A "giver" of "call" money has the right to purchase shares during the three months at today's price; a giver of "put" money has the right to sell, and the giver of "put and call" money has the choice either to buy or to sell.

CALL

For the sake of lucidity, it may be as well to take a hypothetical case, mentioning a price and an amount of option money more or less at random. Suppose that a share stands at £1·49 to £1·51 and you think that it is likely to rise considerably in price but, you wish to limit the amount of a possible loss, or you lack the money to buy and pay for the shares outright, you will consider doing an option. Also, by doing an option, you can control more shares than you could buy outright. You ask your broker to quote a call option rate; he will approach the three option dealers and find that one is willing to "take" £0·12½ per share for the call of . . . shares at £1·51 (the market offered price) plus 2½p contango. This contango rate is added to the offered price and represents the dealer's cost of financing the option over the three month period. You agree, and are said to have given £0·12½ for the call at a "striking price" of £1·53½. (£1·51 plus 2½p contango) for three months. The option money is theoretically due for settlement when the option is exercised or abandoned—but most brokers require settlement at the end of the current account.

The only further expense need be commission which is charged on the number of shares at the striking price. If the option is exercised, and the shares are bought and then sold "to close" in the market, no further commission is payable. However, if they are taken up, government stamp duty is also payable.

The three months' maximum period is not strictly correct; the option must be exercised, for settlement, at latest, on the seventh Account day after the date of doing the option. The day on which it may be exercised during any account up to this time is called "declaration" day and is the penultimate day of dealing for the account.

In the example, at the end of three months, you have the right to buy the shares at £1·53½. The expenses involved are £0·12½ option money plus about 2p commission (1¼ per cent on £1·53½) which totals £1·68. If the price is higher than this, you call the shares at £1.53½, sell them in the market free of expenses, and the difference is your profit. If the market price were between £1·53½ and £1·68, the option would be exercised to salvage part of the outlay.

PUT

Consider the same share at the same price, £1·49 to £1·51 and suppose you take the view that the price is likely to fall heavily in the near future, you do not wish to sell as an un-covered bear, so you give money for the "put" for three months. The option money is usually the same as for the call, although your broker may have a little more difficulty in finding a taker. The striking price in this case is the bid price, £1·49, as there is no contango on put options.

The bargain is done; you have given £0·12½ for the put of . . . shares at £1·49 for three months. You now have the right to put the shares on the option dealer, i.e., to sell them to him at the option price up to the end of three months, irrespective of the market price.

If, at the end of three months, the price is above £1·49, you abandon the option and lose your option money. If the price is between £1·36½ and £1·49 you buy the shares in the market and "put" them to recover part of your option money. If they are offered at less than £1·36½ you make a profit, ignoring commission which is 2p a share. In any case, your loss is limited to the cost of the option.

PUT AND CALL

Consider the same share at £1·49–£1·51 for a third time; you expect news shortly which is likely to affect the price of the share very considerably one way or the other, but you have no idea as to whether the news will be favourable or the reverse. You therefore give for the "put and call" or "double option"; the option money will be twice the single option (£0·25 in our hypothetical case) and the option price, the middle price, namely, £1·50 (or any price agreed between the giver and the option dealer).

The price must rise or fall £0·25 before you can make a profit (unless you job against your option, *see below*) but, as the price is not likely to remain steady for the whole three months, you are not likely to lose the whole of your option money.

JOBBING AGAINST AN OPTION

If, after you have given for the call, the price rises sharply, you sell the shares and "take them in" until you can buy them back more cheaply and then repeat the process, or until the option expires.

Similarly, if, after you have given for the put, the price falls sharply, you buy the shares and "give on them" (carry them over) until you can sell them at a higher price, or until the expiry of the option.

After giving for the double option, you can job against it in this way, whether the price rises or falls.

This brief explanation of options shows that they provide a safe, though rather expensive, way of speculating; they are usually regarded as a means of gambling, though they may also be regarded as a form of insurance.

OPTIONS AS INSURANCE

As an example, let us suppose that you have invested in the ordinary shares of a brewery company (as you very well may have done, since most breweries are well-managed concerns, whose shares make a sound investment). A month or so before the Budget a rumour goes round that the beer duty is to be increased; you feel nervous, but the shares have already fallen slightly, and you do not feel inclined to cut a loss; you might go to Lloyds and insure against an increase in the beer duty, but your simplest plan would probably be to give for the put of your shares for a period long enough to carry you over the Budget. The insurance aspect of options is often overlooked.

Another point to be borne in mind is that, supposing that you feel very strongly that there is going to be a big rise in the price of a certain share in a very short time but you are not willing to put a large sum of money into it, you can take an interest in a far larger number of shares by giving for the call than you can by buying the shares outright.

Suppose the shares stand at £3 and the three months' call is £0·15. Ignoring expenses for the sake of simplicity you could buy 100 shares for £300 but with that amount of money you could give for the call of 2,000 shares. Do not forget, though, that if you bought 100 shares you would at the end of three months still have 100 shares to show for your £300 plus expenses while, unless the price had risen to £3 plus, say, £0·07½ contango, you would have nothing at all to show for the money and, unless the price had risen to over £3·22½ you would not show any profit at all on the option.

The price of an option, like that of anything else, depends on supply and demand. Normally the rate will be between 5 per cent and 10 per cent of the market price depending on the marketability of the share and on how volatile its movements usually are. To quite a large extent the rate quoted by an option dealer will depend on his instinct, born of long experience in this highly specialized form of dealing.

TAKING OPTION MONEY

Just as the bookies make more money than the average punter it is probably more profitable to "take" option money than it is to "give" it, but this can be dangerous unless you know exactly what you are doing and you must have a holding of the particular share and an amount of readily available cash to correspond. To enable you to understand this it is essential to explain option dealing a little more fully.

Suppose that Mr. Smith instructs his broker to give £0·15 for the call of 200 Mild and Bitters; the broker finds that the price is £2·97½ to £3. The option dealer agrees to take £0·15 for the three months' call of 200 Mild and Bitters at £3·07½ (£3 plus 7½p contango), and the bargain is booked. The option dealer may decide to chance his arm and do nothing about it; if the price falls he makes £0·15 a share profit but if there should be a big rise in the price he would make a heavy loss; he might do this if the option is only in a small number of shares but he would really be gambling rather than doing option business.

Normally the option dealer tries to "undo" the business. He might bid a broker £0·14 for the call of 200 Mild and Bitters and the broker, knowing that his client, Mr. Brown, had a large holding, might get him to "take" it. If the price remains steady or falls, the option is "abandoned" and Mr. Brown is paid £0·14 (less commission) on 200 shares and keeps his shares. If at the end of the three months the price has risen to £3·50, Mr. Smith's broker "calls" them from the option dealer at £3·07½ and he in turn "calls" them from Mr. Brown at the same price. The option dealer receives £30 option money (200 times £0·15) and pays out £28 (200 times £0·14). Mr. Brown receives £3·07½ for his shares plus £0·14 option money (£3·21½ in all). He might well have sold 200 of his large holding at that price, in any case, so he is no worse off and has had the chance of receiving £0·14 for taking a risk which did not eventuate.

Another possibility is that having taken £0·15 for the three months' call of 200 Mild and Bitters at £3·07½ the option dealer may buy 100 Mild and Bitters at £3 (or get Mr. Smith's broker to buy them for his, the option dealer's, account). The option dealer will contango these 100 shares for each consecutive account until the option expires. Having bought his 100

Mild and Bitters at £3 the option dealer will then immediately try to find somebody who is willing to "take" £0·28 "put and call" of 100 Mild and Bitters at £3·07½ for three months and we will assume that he is successful, the "taker" being a Mr. Jones.

The option dealer has then assured himself of a profit of 2½p on 100 shares (or 1¼p on 200 shares). It works out as follows—

If on declaration day at 2.45 p.m. (declaration day is the last day but one of dealing for the Account Day for which the option has been done) Mild and Bitters can be sold at £3·07½ or a higher price Mr. Smith "calls" his 200 shares and the option dealer "calls" 100 shares from Mr. Jones. The option dealer delivers to Mr. Smith the 100 shares which he bought originally together with the 100 shares "called" from Mr. Jones, all being paid for at £3·07½. The option dealer receives from Mr. Smith's broker 200 times £0·15 call money (£30) and pays 100 times £0·28 put-and-call money (£28) to Mr. Jones's broker.

If, on the other hand, at declaration time Mild and Bitters can be bought in the market at £3·07½ or lower, Mr. Smith "abandons" his call and the option dealer "puts" the 100 shares, which he originally bought, on Mr. Jones. The option dealer still receives £30 option money and pays out £28 option money as above.

You can always "give" option money on any reasonably active share but you can only "take" for the put and call if your broker can find an option dealer trying to "undo" an option on the particular share in which you are interested; as the option dealer may have "taken" option money a day or two earlier, the "striking price" at which he wishes to deal may be slightly different from the market price at the time at which you deal, but only time will show whether that is to your advantage or disadvantage.

Now put yourself into the position of Mr. Jones in the example just described. You must hold 100 Mild and Bitters and be prepared to keep them for at least three months and you must know that you will have about £300 in cash available in three months' time.

Having "taken" £0·28 "put and call" you have no choice in the matter; you have, in fact, sold to the option dealer the right either to buy 100 shares from you at £3·07½ or to sell 100 shares to you at that price.

Suppose that on declaration day the price of Mild and Bitters has risen to £3·50; the shares will be "called" but in effect you receive £3·35½ for them (£3·07½ plus £0·28 option money) and you may reflect that had you not "taken for the put and call' you would probably have sold them at about £3·35 in any case.

Suppose, on the other hand, that on declaration day Mild and Bitters stand at only £2·50; the shares will be "put" on you at £3·07½ but, as you receive £0·28 option money, they only cost you £2·80, and, as you were content to hold them when they stood at £3, it is not unlikely that you would have bought more at £2·80 on the way down had you not taken for the "put and call".

If the price on declaration day is between £2·80 and £3·35 you would either buy back in the market the shares "called" from you or sell the shares "put" on you, and take as profit the difference between your gross loss and the option money received, and this third possibility is the most likely outcome of the transaction.

Ignoring commission, the price must move more than the amount of the "put and call" money either up or down before the taker actually makes a loss; in the above example there is a spread of £0·55 (from £2·80 to £3·35) within which the taker for the "put and call" makes a profit or at least escapes loss.

Profits made on options are liable to 30 per cent capital gains tax and the option money may be deducted as an expense. However, option money lost on abandoned options is not an allowable loss. A loss incurred by exercising an option and dealing against it may be regarded as an allowable loss and the total loss may be offset against other profits.

CHAPTER XVIII

Take-over Bids

TAKE-OVER BIDS present great problems for brokers because it is often impossible for them to give advice; they can only guess what is likely to happen because such bids fall into so many different categories.

The simplest case is when the directors of Company A hold more than 50 per cent of the voting power and agree irrevocably to accept the terms of the take-over bid by Company B. If the bid is in cash, shareholders in A know where they stand; if, as is more often the case, the bid is partly in shares in Company B and partly in Company B's loan stock or convertible loan stock, A's shareholders have to guess what the prices of those shares and loans will be when they are actually issued. The fear that those holders of Company A who do not want Company B's shares will be sellers, may well have a depressing effect on the share price of Company B.

In a rising market it may pay shareholders in Company A to sell at once slightly below the ostensible value of the bid in order to be able to re-invest at once rather than wait for perhaps a couple of months before receiving their cash or new securities.

Another variety is when the directors of Company A hold a substantial amount, say 30 per cent of the shares and make a firm commitment to accept a bid from Company B for their own shares and to recommend acceptance by the other shareholders on the grounds that the bid is reasonable, is above the market price and that they see no likelihood of obtaining a better bid. They then find themselves in a quandary when the directors of Company C, possibly sparked off by the bid from Company B, make a better bid; they cannot go back on their word which was probably given in perfectly good faith. Shareholders can only guess whether B or C will win and will probably be well advised to sell in the market if they can get a better price than the value of B's bid.

If a company is offering its own shares as currency and is forced to increase its offer, each successive raising of the terms quite often results in a weakening of its own share price; this of course reduces the value of the bid, bringing a return to near square one. In order to avoid this, a profits forecast or other bullish statement will often accompany the raising of an offer.

Nevertheless, it can pay to await the outcome of an auction, especially if the two companies, fighting for control of a third, each seems determined to be the victor.

There have been several cases of a quite different sort. The directors of Company A have been violently opposed to the company being taken over and have produced forecasts of the current year's profits which have resulted in defeating the take-over bid. In at least one case the directors have failed lamentably to produce anything like the profits which they so confidently forecast and their shareholders are far worse off than they would have been if they had accepted the bid. The Take-over Panel now insist on such forecasts being examined by independent accountants but, even so, it seems that these forecasts should be taken with several grains of salt.

Another category is where a small company, A, makes a bid for another company, B, which is much bigger than itself in terms of market capitalization. This has been nicknamed a "shell" operation. Quite often, Company A will be in a completely different line of business from Company B, and the shares of Company A may well stand at a considerable premium over their asset value. This often means that the management of Company A consists of shrewd business men who hope to be able to improve the earnings of Company B, whose management is sluggish, or maybe they consider that they can break up the company's assets and realize more than the bid price.

This premium over the asset value of Company A's shares reflects the investor's willingness to discount tomorrow's beneficial acquisitions today. One must beware of these inflated prices because a big fall in the price of Company A's shares will occur if the management does not live up to the market's expectations.

The following chapters are mainly for students, although the general reader will find them informative.

CHAPTER XIX

Arbitrage

CONSIDER a number of tanks of water connected below the water-line by narrow-bore pipes. If water is removed from one tank or, if water is added to another, the water levels in each tank will be different but after a time, the levels in all the tanks will again become the same.

In much the same way, the price levels of any securities normally dealt in in different countries will find their own level and this process is assisted, or accelerated, by Arbitrage. Arbitrage is defined as the business of buying or selling a security as a Principal in one centre with the intention of reversing such a transaction in a centre (or country) other than that in which the original transaction took place in order to profit from the price difference between the two centres.

Both brokers and jobbers may engage in Arbitrage, but a broker must keep his ordinary business quite separate from his Arbitrage business, while a jobber may only Arbitrage on Joint Account with his foreign correspondent and only in those securities in which he normally deals.

Arbitrage is a very specialized business because the arbitrageur must take account not only of prices but also of rates of exchange and of the fact that dealings in London are for the account while in many foreign countries they are for cash; further, he must consider the cost of sending bearer securities abroad, including insurance and the time taken in transit.

A broker who wishes to arbitrage on Joint Account must apply for annual authorization from the Council. (Appendix 32.)

Shunting. This is virtually the same thing as arbitrage except that it is carried out in this country with a member of a Federated Stock Exchange and annual authorization from the Council is required. (Appendix 32d).

CHAPTER XX

Australian Shares

T HE 1969/70 boom in Australian mining shares raised a number of difficulties, but companies such as Ampol Petroleum, Broken Hill Proprietary, Broken Hill South and North Broken Hill, which maintain London as well as Australian registers, were not affected.

These difficulties stemmed from several different causes—

(*a*) The time taken to despatch and return documents to and from Australia.

(*b*) Australian company registrars, geared to dealing with a few transfers a week, were quite unable to cope with the flood of transfers with which they were suddenly faced. This is the main source of trouble. It has affected mining shares but not industrial shares, dealings in which have not greatly increased in volume.

(*c*) Australian practice is different from that of London; in particular, "certification" and "renounceable" documents are unknown.

(*d*) Instead, the company issues letters of rights to shareholders, enabling them to take up new shares. If they wish to renounce the new shares, a separate form is required but it can only be used after the new shares have been taken up. Thus, in Australia, the registered shareholder has to take up and pay for the rights, if they are not to lapse, even if he is no longer the beneficial owner, having sold his shares before the date of the rights issue; if the new beneficial owner has not yet been registered, it is difficult, if not impossible, for him, successfully, to claim his rights.

(*e*) When a client of a London broker buys shares in a company which only maintains an Australian register and sells part or all of them within a short time, he is unable to deliver them until he has received the certificate for the purchase from Australia and this may take many months. Brokers are, therefore, obliged to demand immediate payment for purchases, but are not in a position to pay for sales until delivery is effected, possibly many months later, much to the annoyance and dismay of the client.

(*f*) In order to reduce some of these delays, the market agreed only to deal in round amounts of shares as follows—

Price		Multiples of
Up to	12$\frac{1}{2}$p	1,000
12$\frac{1}{2}$p	to 25p	500
25p	to 50p	100
Over	50p	50

(*g*) Registrars of United Kingdom companies send certificates to the stockbrokers who lodged the transfers for registration and only despatch, direct to the shareholder, certificates resulting from a capitalization issue. In Australia, registrars normally send certificates direct to the shareholder.

(*h*) Brokers in London usually arrange for the registration of transfers in Australia to be carried out by one of the Australian banks or by an Australian broker. It is also quite usual to have Australian shares registered in the name of the nominee company of an Australian bank and held, in Australia, to the order of the client's bank in the United Kingdom.

The Australian authorities may however adopt some of the well-tried techniques practised in London in order to make business between the two countries run more smoothly.

It was announced in April, 1970, that it is hoped to eliminate the delays in obtaining certificates for shares in Australian companies and the consequential time lag in obtaining payment when such shares are sold soon after purchase, by the introduction of the Bearer Deposit Receipt scheme. The BDR scheme should also greatly reduce the risk of the buyer losing his entitlement to rights issues.

Buyers will be able to instruct their brokers to obtain their shares in the form of BDRs at an extra cost of about one per cent.

The relevant documents will be obtained fairly quickly by an

Authorized Depositary, e.g. the Bank of New South Wales, which will hold them and secure dividends, rights offers, and scrip issues for the buyer.

This scheme is supported by such influential companies as the English Association of American Bond and Shareholders, the National Bank of Australasia and the Australia and New Zealand Banking Group.

At present the scheme covers a number of companies such as Allied Mills, Bell Bros., Carlton and United Breweries, Colonial Sugar Refining, Dunlop Australia, Myer Emporium and several mining companies and it is rapidly expanding.

CHAPTER XXI

Buying-In and Selling-Out

WHEN a broker cannot obtain delivery of shares which he has bought, he has recourse to the Buying-in and Selling-Out Department of the Stock Exchange.

Similarly, when the buyer failed to provide the ultimate seller with a "name" to enable him to deliver the securities and receive payment, the selling broker could "sell-out for a name."

Buying-in. Registered securities may be bought-in, on, or after the 10th day after Account Day; bearer securities may be bought in, on, or after the third business day after Account Day.

Twenty-four hours' notice, to be posted in the Stock Exchange before 12.30 p.m., is required. On the next business day, between 1.30 and 3.0 p.m., an official of the Buying-In and Selling-Out Department openly bids for the security in the market.

If the stock is sold to him, any loss incurred is the liability of the ultimate seller, unless he can prove that the delay was caused by a late ticket in which case the liability is borne by the firm at fault.

If, as usually happens, no seller appears, Buying-In takes place daily until the instructions are countermanded.

In addition to paying for any loss incurred, the offending broker has to pay the Buying-In Department full commission on the first day, whether successful or not, and half commission on each subsequent day.

In addition, it must be remembered that the offender, provided that Buying-In against him has been successful, is left as a "stale bull" since his buyer has been satisfied from another source.

A Member who sells to the Buying-In Department Official must deliver the stock on the following business day.

The threat to Buy-In often produces delivery of the stock.

Brokers are very reluctant to Buy-In because the procedure is rarely successful and always generates ill-will. Its main purpose is to show the client that every effort is being made to secure delivery of his stock.

No broker will Buy-In against jobbers, other than in exceptional circumstances, because he is unwilling to penalize them for selling short, possibly against their better judgment, in order to oblige him or some other broker; jobbers help brokers (and, through them, help their clients) in many ways and it would be folly to forfeit such help by antagonizing them.

Selling-out. This never happens with "cash" stocks because delivery can be made to the immediate buyer on the business day after the sale.

When the name and address of the transferee had to appear on the ticket, so that the ultimate seller could prepare the transfer, "late" tickets might result from lack of instructions from the client.

Now that the seller need only know whether all the shares sold are to go on one transfer, or whether they are to go on two or more transfers, "late" tickets occur less frequently. Until he receives the ticket(s), the selling broker cannot tell whether he is to stamp the stock transfer or to have broker's transfers prepared, certified and stamped, neither does he know from whom to claim payment against delivery.

Selling-Out for a Name may take place between 2.30 p.m. and 3.0 p.m. on the First Intermediate Day (the day after tickets are "passed") or between 11.0 a.m. and 3.0 p.m. on any subsequent business day.

The actual "Selling-Out" is done by an official of the Buying-In & Selling-Out Department going into the market and offering the stock in a kind of Dutch Auction, reducing the price until a buyer appears. The Member to whom the Buying-In and Selling-Out Department has sold the stock must provide the Department with a ticket within half-an-hour.

The original buyer who has failed to pass a ticket before 3 p.m. on Ticket Day is liable for any loss incurred by the seller, and must pay commission on the sale to the Buying-In and Selling-Out Department. He is left a bear of the stock, unless he can prove that there has been undue delay on the trace.

A ticket may pass through many hands and each member

records the time of receipt on the back; the ticket can be traced back "on the trace" and the member responsible for the delay in issuing the ticket, or for passing it on, is liable for all the loss and expense incurred.

If the member who buys the stock from the Buying-In and Selling-Out Department fails to pass a ticket within half-an-hour, the stock is again "Sold-Out"—this time, against him.

The advent of the Computerized Inter-Firm Accounting System which, at the time of writing, is in experimental use, will presumably ensure the issue of tickets in good time and so make Selling-Out unnecessary; if there should be delay in issuing a ticket it will be due to electronic or mechanical break-down, thus making the allocation of blame and, consequently, of financial liability, virtually impossible.

CHAPTER XXII

Ex Dividend

REGISTERED gilt-edged stocks are made ex dividend on the last day on which transfers can be registered "cum dividend."

Gilt-edged bargains are for settlement on the following business day; transfers in respect of bargains made cum dividend should, therefore, be registered in time for the buyer to receive the dividend direct.

Bargains made (ex dividend) on the day on which the "books are closed" are not due for settlement until the following day by which time transfers can only be registered ex dividend.

Registered securities other than gilt-edged (except Registered Debentures) and securities which are dealt in both in bearer and in registered form, are made ex dividend on the Preliminary Day before the Account Day preceding the last day on which transfers can be registered cum dividend.

That is to say that if all sales are delivered on Account Day and the buyers, to whom they are delivered, register them promptly, all cum dividend buyers will receive the dividend direct from the company.

Bargains done on the Preliminary Day (the first day of dealing for the new account) are due for settlement one Account Day later, by which time the transfer books will have been closed.

If the Quotations Department is not informed in time, the price will be made ex dividend on the following Preliminary Day unless that is later than the date of payment of the dividend. The price must be made ex dividend on or before the date of the dividend payment.

It must be noted that the exception does not apply to registered debenture stock; the probable reason is that "debentures" were bearer bonds (made ex dividend on date of payment) which were registered as a security measure during the 1939/45 war.

Whatever the denomination of these debentures (£500, £100 for example), they cannot be sub-divided and must be transferred "in toto"; transfer is by deed but no new certificate is issued; the company merely draws a line through the name of the previous holder (the transferor) and enters the name and address of the transferee on the back of the debenture.

The fact that there are very few of these debentures probably explains why this relic of the past has been allowed to remain; it would simplify procedure if they were brought into line with the rest of the registered securities.

Bearer securities which are not also dealt in in registered form, and registered debentures, are made ex dividend on the day on which the dividend is due to be paid. However, if the coupons are only payable abroad, the price may be made ex dividend on the Preliminary Day which allows time for transmission of the coupon for payment on the due date.

Shares in "American form" are made ex dividend on the business day after they have been made ex dividend in America or Canada.

The basis of the ex dividend rules is to ensure that the dividend or interest payment is made to the person entitled to it with the least delay and with as little trouble as possible.

CHAPTER XXIII

Central Inter-Firm Accounting

NEW Rules, deliberately designated as "Temporary," since they may have to be modified in light of experience, were introduced in January, 1970.

The Stock Exchange dealing day now runs from 5 p.m. until 5 p.m. on the next business day and a normal fortnightly account runs from 5 p.m. on Friday, the last day of dealing for the old account, until 5 p.m. on Friday, a fortnight later.

It is convenient here to substitute "First Monday," "final Thursday" and "final Friday" for "the first day of dealing for the New Account," "the penultimate day of dealing for the Old Account" and "the last day of dealing for the Old Account"; the sense is clear although when dealing for a new account happens to start on the Thursday before Good Friday or on the Friday before the Autumn Bank Holiday, the necessary adjustments must be made.

A bargain done at 5.15 p.m. on Tuesday will, for accounting purposes, be deemed to have been done on Wednesday and the contract must be dated "Wednesday."

Similarly, a bargain done after 5 p.m. on the final Friday is deemed to have been done on the first Monday of the New Account and is therefore automatically done for the New Account.

Bargains done after 5 p.m. must be "cum dividend" or "cum rights" even if the price is to be made ex dividend or ex rights on the next business day.

As the Rule stands, there will be nothing in the books of account to show whether the bargain was done late on the Friday "cum dividend" or on the first Monday "ex dividend." To avoid any doubt, at least one firm types "p.d." (post-dated) on all contracts referring to late afternoon bargains and some such practice will probably be made obligatory.

No business may be done in new issues before 9.30 a.m. on

the day on which permission to deal has been granted. Dealings "for New Time" are allowed on the last two days of dealing for the old account and are also permissible after 5.00 p.m. on the previous day.

The first Monday used to be called "Contango Day" but is now known as "Preliminary Day" because all contangos now have to be arranged on the final Friday. Brokers may only do contangos with jobbers; jobbers must advise brokers immediately after 4.30 p.m. on the final Friday whether or not the contangos have been done.

Brokers then have until 6.30 p.m. to close transactions done for the current Account or deals which have been thrown out.

No contangos or cash bargains to close "frustrated" contangos may be made after 6.30 p.m. on the final Friday.

The "Making-Up" prices for contangos are the middle market prices at the close of the Exchange on the final Thursday.

INTER-FIRM ACCOUNTING[1]

This falls into two parts—

(1) Recording and checking bargains, working out and recording considerations to be credited or debited to each firm;

(2) Recording deliveries to the Central Office by firms which have sold securities; sorting them out for collection by the firms which have bought them and paying out or claiming the balance for the day.

The ticket must be issued at the price paid by the buyer who is to pay for the securities and take them up at the end of the account so that the proper stamp duty can be charged; except by coincidence this will be different from the price received by the seller who is to deliver them; the differences mentioned below are the sum of the profits and losses made by the jobbers and brokers through whose hands the shares have passed during the account.

Part 1.

All firms must supply the Central Accounting Office with copies of that part of all contract notes showing—

---

[1] Inter-Firm Accounting has proved too complex for the Stock Exchange computer and the system has been temporarily shelved.

(a) the name and code number of the firm with which the bargain was done
(b) the code number of the security
(c) the amount of stock or the number of shares bought or sold
(d) the price at which the deal took place.

A charge is made for each item handled: the copies can be handed in in batches and the earlier in the day the batch is handed in, the smaller the charge per item.

The wording of a contract note is as set out in the specimen contracts on page 25 but, in practice, the form is different. All contracts are now typed with a number of carbon copies, including the Journal Sheet; it is, therefore, convenient to set the figures out horizontally. The contracts are on forms printed on different coloured paper for bought and sold contracts, in order to avoid mistakes, with a BOUGHT or SOLD in large letters near the top.

There are spaces for the name of the client and for the date of the bargain and the date of settlement; below are columns, headed as follows from left to right; they are here described as columns because that is how they appear on the Journal Sheet after a number of contracts have been typed, although there may be, and very often is, only one figure in each column of the contract. The headings are—

Jobber (on a perforated slip which is torn off before the contract is sent out)
Amount
Security
Price
Consideration
Commission (Rate)
Commission(Amount)
Contract stamp
Transfer stamp
Transfer fee (usually called Registration fee)
Total

On a sold contract the transfer stamp and fee columns are only used on the rare occasions when a sale is made "free of transfer expenses"; such bargains are virtually obsolete as they upset the accounting system; instead, when a small broken amount has to be sold, it is usual to accept a price below the market price and this comes more or less to the same thing.

Carbon copies of part or all of the contract note go to the Inter-Firm Accounting to be fed into the computer, to the checking clerk, and to the clerks who keep the clients' and jobbers' ledgers.

These contracts are fed into a computer which is programmed to ignore, except for the purpose of checking and of compiling a statistical record of the volume of daily business, all bargains done for cash, i.e. mainly "gilt-edged" but also renounceable allotment letters and certificates.

The computer extends each bargain and supplies each firm on the following business day with a statement showing—

> Name and code number of the jobber (or broker) with whom the business was done
> Amount and name of security
> Whether bought or sold
> Price
> Consideration debited (bought bargain) or credited (sold bargain)
> Total consideration for all purchases made that day
> Amount brought forward from the previous days (if any) of the current Account
> The total for the account so far.
> Similar totals for all sales.

At the end of the Account, if the purchase considerations exceed the sales, the firm will pay the difference to the Central Office; if the sales exceed the purchases, the firm will receive the difference.

Instead of checking bargains with the jobber or broker, the checking clerk checks them with the computer statement.

It must be noted that only the considerations appear on these statements which do not include commissions or stamp duties.

Part 2

The SETTLEMENT PERIOD consists of seven business

days calculated backwards from the Account Day which is always a Tuesday. These are—

Preliminary Day (Monday). This is always the first day of dealing for the new account and is always a Monday unless a Bank Holiday intervenes. Tickets in respect of purchases are prepared on this day and also on the—

Making-Up Day (Tuesday). Traditionally, prices on the previous day were collected and used for calculating contangos. As explained above, contangos are now done on the Friday. Making-Up prices for use with Clearing Stocks are also taken on the previous day.

Ticket Day (Wednesday), is the day on which brokers pass tickets which they prepared during the previous two days.

First Intermediate Day (Thursday)

Second Intermediate Day (Friday)

These two days are used for passing tickets received on to other brokers, where necessary.

Third Intermediate Day (Monday). The day before Account Day; some tickets may still be passing between brokers.

Account Day (Tuesday)

The buying broker issues a "Ticket" showing the amount of stock or number of shares and the name and description of the security, the price, consideration and stamp duty and the total; the printed ticket ends up with ". . . . . . . (name of the firm) and . . . (its code number) pay", by putting it in the box in the Central Office of the firm from whom he bought the security.

The selling broker eventually receives the ticket which may have been split on the way. He pins the ticket to the transfer and certificate, or to the certified transfer, and delivers them to the Central Office.

Central Office sorts these deliveries for collection by the buyers.

Selling brokers must provide the Central Office with a daily list showing what has been delivered and the total amount claimed (considerations plus stamps) and receive a cheque in payment.

The Central Office lists the securities put out for each firm (the buyers) to collect and sends each firm a debit note which must be paid at once.

In order to obtain payment on Account Day, securities may be delivered to Central Office on the previous day but not later than 3.30 p.m. Thereafter, securities delivered by 11.30 a.m. will be paid for on the same day.

The client who buys securities pays for the transfer stamp but the selling broker actually pays the Inland Revenue to stamp the transfer and is paid on delivery by the buying broker. The time-consuming process of having transfers stamped by the Inland Revenue is likely to be abolished before long; instead, the Stock Exchange will collect the stamp duty from the buyer and pay the Inland Revenue a lump sum at the end of each account.

CHAPTER XXIV

City Code on Take-Overs and Mergers

REFERENCE was made in Chapter I to the report of the Royal Commission, set up in 1877, which concluded that the Stock Exchange Rules were "capable of affording relief and exercising restraint far more prompt and often more satis-factory than any within reach of the Courts of Law" and to the Cohen Commission's opinion that the Stock Exchange regula-tions could be made more stringent than the Law because, since they lacked statutory authority, they could be waived or relaxed when the merits of individual cases warranted it.

It is in the same spirit that it is generally accepted that a system of voluntary self-discipline based on the Code is likely to be more practicable and more efficient than regulation by law.

As was noted in Chapter III, in order to avoid misunder-standings in the Stock Market, a would-be buyer of shares always "bids" for them, while a would-be seller "offers" his shares. The Press normally mentions "take-over bids" and it is therefore, rather sad that the Panel uses the inelegant and potentially misleading "offeror" instead of "bidder" and the equally inelegant "offeree"; it is admitted that a suitable alternative to "offeree" is not easy to find but "tendered" company might do, or the more clumsy "object of the bid."

The Code is administered by the Panel on Take-Overs and Mergers, The Stock Exchange Building, London E.C.2 and copies of the Code can be obtained from the Secretary.

The Panel consider it impractical to devise rules to cover all the different circumstances likely to arise in take-over or merger transactions and, therefore, stress the importance of compliance with the spirit of the regulations by all interested parties.

The rules have been framed so as to ensure as far as possible that—

(1) No person privy to the preliminary take-over or merger

discussions is allowed to have dealings of any kind (including option business) in the shares of either side after the initial approach has been made or intimated or, that there is reason to suppose that such an approach will be made and before the approach or the bid has been made public or before the discussions have been terminated.

(2) Absolute secrecy should be maintained until the news is published.

(3) In any situation likely to lead to a take-over bid, whether welcome or not, a close watch should be kept on the share market and, in the event of any untoward movement in the prices of the shares concerned, an immediate announcement with any appropriate comment must be made.

(4) When the Board is notified of a firm intention from a serious source to make a bid, shareholders must be informed at once by a notice in the press which should be followed as soon as possible by a circular. The identity of the bidder must be disclosed and the company making the bid must disclose how many shares in the company for which it is bidding it holds or controls, directly or indirectly through associates.

(5) Directors must act in the interest of all shareholders and when they hold what amounts to a controlling interest, they must be particularly careful to examine their motives, especially when recommending acceptance of the lower of two bids or the rejection of a bid. They must be prepared to justify their good faith in the interests of the shareholders as a whole. (Presumably they must also consider the interests of their employees).

(6) There are obvious dangers in announcing prematurely an approach which may be withdrawn. However, the facts should be announced as soon as the two companies have reached a basic agreement and are reasonably confident that the negotiations will be successful.

(7) Joint statements are desirable but both companies are equally responsible for making the announcement.

(8) Once the directors are aware of the imminence of a *bona fide* bid, they are precluded from taking any action, without shareholders' approval, to frustrate the bid, or to deny the shareholders an opportunity to decide on its merits.

(9) When approached with a bid, the Board should immediately seek competent advice—usually from a Merchant Bank.

(10) Once the announcement has been made the Board should circularize their shareholders with the fullest possible information in support of their recommendation either to accept or to reject the bid. The directors are individually and collectively responsible for considering all statements of facts and opinions contained in the circular and for ensuring that no material facts or considerations have been omitted.

(11) Profit forecasts are the responsibility of the directors but accounting bases and calculations for the forecasts must be examined by the auditors or consulting accountants who must state, in writing, that they have given and have not withdrawn their consent to the publication of their report. A similar statement from the financial adviser must be given.

(12) Documents sent to shareholders must be prepared with the same standard of care that is applicable to a Prospectus under the Companies Act, 1948.

(13) The directors of both companies must disclose both the Company's and their personal holdings in either Company, (a Company cannot, of course, hold its own shares) and, as regards their own beneficial shareholdings, the Directors of the Company receiving the bid must state whether or not they intend to accept it.

(14) Where the bid is partly or entirely for cash, the bid document must include confirmation, by an independent party, that adequate resources are available.

(15) It must be a condition of a bid that, if successful, it will give voting control to the bidder, and that the bid will not be declared unconditional unless more than 50 per cent of the voting rights have been acquired. This includes shares held before the bid.

(16) The bid must be open for at least 21 days after documents have been posted and, if revised, it must be kept open for at least 8 days after the revision notification has been posted to shareholders.

(17) An acceptor shall be entitled to withdraw his acceptance after the expiry of 21 days after the first closing date of the bid if it has not by then been declared unconditional; the right of withdrawal continues until the bid becomes, or is declared, unconditional.

(18) If a company announces a bid but fails to proceed with

the formal bid within a reasonable period of time it must be prepared to justify itself to the Panel.

(19) Unless a counter bid has occurred, a formal bid may not be withdrawn during its currency without the permission of the Panel.

(20) After a bid has become or been declared unconditional, it must remain open for at least 14 days unless it became unconditional on an expiry date and ten days' written notice had been given that the bid would not remain open beyond that date.

(21) By 9.30 a.m. on the business day following the expiry of the bid, or of the extended or revised bid, the bidder must announce and simultaneously inform the Stock Exchange that—

(a) the bid has become or is declared unconditional and, if so, the total number of shares,
   (i) for which the bid has been accepted,
   (ii) held before the bid,
   (iii) acquired or agreed to be agreed to be acquired during the bid period,
or (b) the bid has been allowed to lapse.

(22) If the bidding company fails to comply with any of these requirements, the Stock Exchange will consider suspending dealings in shares in either or both companies.

(23) If the bidding company, having declared an offer unconditional, fails by 3.30 p.m. on the relevant day to comply with the requirements, the unconditional declaration shall be void.

(24) Bids for a part of the equity not held by the bidder are generally undesirable but, if they can be justified, they must enable shareholders in the company to be taken over to accept in full for the relevant portion of their holdings.

(25) A partial bid which would not give the bidder voting control may not be made without the consent of the Panel and such a bid may not be declared unconditional unless acceptances are received for the total number of shares for which the bid is made. In some circumstances these conditions may be waived by the Panel.

DEALINGS

(26) It has not been considered practicable to define an "Associate" in precise terms but it may include parent or subsidiary companies of either the bidding company or the object of the bid, the directors (and their close relatives and related trusts) of either company, the bankers and stockbrokers who normally act for the companies concerned, the pension funds of those companies and any company or individual holding or acquiring 10 per cent or more of the equity of either company.

As it is undesirable to fetter the market, all parties to the proposed take-over or merger and their associates are free to deal at arm's length, subject to daily disclosure to the Stock Exchange, the Panel, and the Press, by noon on the business day following the transaction of the total of all shares of either company bought or sold in the market or otherwise by them or their associates for their own account on any day during the bid period and at what average price.

(27) In addition, purchase and sales in either company made by associates on behalf of investment clients who are not themselves associates, must be reported to the Stock Exchange and the Panel but need not be reported to the Press.

(28) In the case of a partial bid, the bidding company and its associates are precluded from dealing in the shares of the offeree company for their own account during the bid period.

(29) Where a partial bid has become unconditional with less than 50 per cent, the bidding company and its associates are precluded from buying shares in the offeree company for their own account during the twelve months starting on the last day of the bid period without the specific agreement of the Panel.

(30) If, during the bid period, the bidding company acquires shares above the bid price (being the final bid price in the event of the original price being raised), then it must pay an increased price to all acceptors, calculated on the weighted average price (excluding buying expenses) of the shares so acquired.

(31) Since dealings by either company or its associates may frustrate or affect the outcome of a bid, the Panel should be

consulted in advance or, if this is not done, the company must be prepared to satisfy the Panel that such action has not prejudiced holders of shares in either company.

Changes of Situation of a Company during a bid.

(32) The Board of an offeree company, knowing that a *bona fide* has been made or is imminent, must not, except in pursuance of an existing contract, without the approval of shareholders in general meeting, issue new equity capital (including convertible stocks etc.), buy or sell assets of material amount or enter into contracts other than in the ordinary course of business. The Panel's consent must be obtained, if an obligation is thought to exist, although no formal contract has been made.

SANCTIONS

(33) If there is a breach of the Code, the Panel can make a private or public censure and, in more flagrant cases, take action to deprive the offender temporarily or permanently of his ability to enjoy the facilities of the securities markets.

(34) The Stock Exchanges have disciplinary powers over their members.

The executive of the Issuing Houses Association are taking powers to suspend or expel a member; such action would not, in law, prevent the issuing house concerned from continuing in business but would severely damage its reputation.

During the bid period the Panel may request the Council of the Stock Exchange to suspend quotation of any security involved or to refuse quotation for any new securities to be issued in connection with an acquisition. In a take-over where Exchange Control is involved, the Panel will maintain close consultation with the Bank of England.

(35) When disciplinary action is proposed, the party concerned can either accept the finding of the Panel, or appeal to an Appeal Committee which will be presided over by Lord Pearce, and will consist of three members of the Panel who did not attend the first hearing, one of them representing the City body (if any) to which the alleged offender belongs.

From time to time a leak of confidential information about a forthcoming take-over bid or new issue occurs. This is of course to be regretted, but the high level of integrity prevalent in the City is proved by the rarity of such occurrences especially when one remembers that, in addition to the principals involved such as the directors of the companies and their auditors, brokers, and solicitors, much of the information is shared by clerks, typists and printers.

CHAPTER XXV

Quotation and Permission to Deal

THE main concern of the Stock Exchange Council is that adequate information should be available at the earliest possible moment to shareholders, or the potential subscribers to a new issue to enable them to form a reasonable estimate of the value of the securities and to prevent a false market from developing.

When a quotation is sought, the brokers to the company are responsible for making the application and for ensuring that all the requisite documents are supplied in good time to the Quotations Department of the Stock Exchange. Finally, the partner who has supervised the work necessary on the application must wait on the meeting of the Committee at which the application is to be considered and be ready to answer questions. If he has done his work properly, all the questions will have been answered in advance and he will not be called upon for any further information.

The list of documents to be submitted for approval and conditions to be fulfilled can be found in Appendix 34 to the Rules and Regulations of the Stock Exchange. The list is too long to be reproduced here but, apart from the formal application signed by the broker and supported by the signatures of at least two firms of jobbers who are prepared to deal in the securities, it includes proofs of the prospectus (to be lodged at least fourteen days before publication) and a final copy of the prospectus signed by all the directors, proofs of all renounceable allotment letters and specimens of the definitive Certificate of Incorporation, Board resolutions authorizing the issue of the securities and of the prospectus and of letters, reports, and valuations from experts with their written consent to publication in the prospectus.

The list also includes the general undertaking to be discussed later and an undertaking to submit the declaration in due course. The fee for quotation must be paid by the brokers before the date of the hearing of the application.

For obvious reasons the declaration cannot be made immediately but it must be made as soon as possible; amongst other things it states that all necessary documents have been filed with the Registrar of Companies, that the Company has received all money due to it from the issue, and that completion of purchase of property shown in the prospectus has taken place and the purchase consideration has been satisfied in cash or in securities.

The declaration also states that definitive certificates have been delivered, or are ready for delivery, and that the shares/debentures, etc., for each class for which quotation exists are identical. Until renounceable securities cease to be renounceable (usually about three weeks after becoming fully paid, or of issue, if issued in fully paid form), they are not identical with the existing securities of the same class.

When new ordinary shares are issued they may rank for dividend with the existing shares but, if issued towards the end of the company's financial year, the terms of the issue may state that the new shares will not rank for any dividend declared in respect of that financial year but will rank *pari passu* with the existing shares for all future dividends.

When a new fixed interest security is issued the terms state the amount per cent payable at the next interest date; this amount is calculated at the appropriate rate per annum on the amounts paid up from the dates on which the calls fall due to the interest payment date.

The new securities become identical with the existing securities when they have ceased to be renounceable and when the prices have been made ex dividend; until that time the new securities are printed in italics in the Official List. In some cases it is not possible to make the necessary declaration until some months after the issue.

Finally, the declaration, signed by a director and the company secretary, must state that in their opinion there are no other facts bearing on the application which ought to be disclosed to the Stock Exchange.

It can be seen that a formidable array of documents is required. The preparation of most of these is the responsibility of the Board of directors, the solicitors, accountants, valuers, advertising agents and printers employed by the company but it is the task of the brokers to the issue to ensure that all these documents are lodged with the Quotations Department in plenty of time and to arrange an amicable settlement of all the differences of opinion which are bound to arise as to the exact wording of documents and of the necessity, or otherwise, of publishing information which the Stock Exchange considers ought to be available to shareholders and which the directors consider ought to be withheld from their trade competitors.

Tact and persistence are the most important qualities required by the brokers and the partner handling the issue must try to anticipate questions or objections likely to be raised by the Quotations Department. He can also save valuable time by lodging documents in person, pointing out anything likely to raise a question and explaining why this, that, or the other has been included or omitted. He should also spot obvious errors in the proofs and, after consultation with the company secretary, amend them before lodging the documents.

THE GENERAL UNDERTAKING

This document is brought up to date from time to time in the light of experience; when a company, which has not signed the general undertaking for some considerable time, seeks quotation for a new issue, it is usually asked to sign the current form of general undertaking.

This binds the company—

(1) To notify the Quotations Department without delay of—

(a) Dates of Board Meetings to declare or to recommend dividends or, to announce profits or losses.

(b) Dividends or bonuses declared, recommended, or passed and preliminary profits for the year and half year.

(c) Certain acquisitions or realization of assets.

(d) Information which the City Take-Over Code requires to be disclosed to the Stock Exchange.

(e) Changes in the directorate, proposed changes in the nature of business or in the beneficial ownership of voting control.

(*f*) Extension of time for the currency of temporary documents, intention to make a drawing of redeemable securities with details of dates, amounts to be drawn and amount outstanding thereafter.

(2) To submit for the Department's prior approval circulars to shareholders, notices of meetings (excepting those dealing with routine business), forms of Proxy and notices by advertisement to holders of bearer securities and to provide copies of these circulars, reports etc., at the same time as they are issued to shareholders, together with resolutions passed by the company other than routine business.

To circularize shareholders within six months of the date of the notice calling the Annual General Meeting, a half-yearly interim report and to include with the annual report a description of the company's activities, split, where appropriate, either by figures or percentages, into different trading categories and geographically, together with the names and location of subsidiary or associated companies and the extent of the parent company's interest therein.

To disclose beneficial interests, waivers of emoluments, service contracts and dealings in shares of the company by directors.

To provide for two-way voting on all resolutions when issuing proxy forms. To obtain the consent of equity shareholders in general meeting before making an issue for cash to other than equity shareholders.

These, and certain other clauses in the General Undertaking, are matters of principle.

(3) Other clauses which are equally important, are concerned with technical details; they bind the company—

(*a*) To insert notices to appear in the press at latest on the morning after allotment letters have been posted showing the basis of allotment in prospectus and other offers and of excess shares.

(*b*) To certify transfers against certificates or temporary documents and return them on the day of receipt.

(*c*) To split and return renounceable documents on the day of receipt.

(*d*) To register transfers and other documents e.g., grants of probate without fee.

(*e*) To issue, without charge, definitive certificates within—

    (i) one month of the last day for renunciation.

    (ii) fourteen days of the lodgement of transfers.

(*f*) To arrange for designated accounts on request.

(*g*) When the company is empowered to issue share warrants to Bearer (i) to issue such warrants within 14 days of the deposit of the share certificates, (ii) to certify transfers against the deposit of warrants to bearer.

CHARGES FOR QUOTATION

In the case of companies seeking quotation in respect of prospectuses, offers for sale, placings, introductions, rights, vendor considerations, the charges vary at present from nil where the value does not exceed £4,999 to 50 guineas where it lies between £50,000 and £100,000; 100 guineas between £100,000 and £200,000; on a sliding scale until a charge of £5,000 guineas where the money value exceeds £75 million.

Capitalization issues, conversions and further issues of identical securities are charged at one half the above scale.

There is also an annual charge of 100 guineas for each company, Corporation or Authority.

There is another scale for British Funds, British Corporation and County and Commonwealth stocks.

CHAPTER XXVI

The Broker to the Company

WHEN a public company seeks a Stock Exchange quotation for existing securities or for new shares to be issued by offer for sale, by capitalization of reserves or as a rights issue for cash, the broker to the company acts as intermediary between the company and its solicitors and the Quotations Department of the Stock Exchange Council.

In addition to some knowledge of Company Law, the broker needs a considerable amount of tact because, although the matter may be perfectly straightforward, the company and its solicitors look at it from one point of view, whereas the Quotations Department view it from a completely different angle; the broker's job is to demonstrate to each side in turn how reasonable the arguments of the other side really are and, eventually, to obtain a compromise acceptable to both.

The broker to a company ought to be able to foresee most of the objections or queries likely to be raised by the Quotations Department and to discuss them with the company or its solicitors in advance; these matters are usually urgent particularly when a document has to be printed and issued by a certain date.

It is exceedingly rare for a company and/or the solicitors to give the broker a reasonable amount of time in which to obtain the Quotations Department's approval. The company knows that it does not take long to read a fairly short document even if it has to be read very critically; it does not wish to know that similar documents by the dozen are being submitted at the same time and all cannot be read simultaneously. Also, certain circulars require approval by the Quotations Department before they may be issued.

A tactful broker can often save time, particularly when the Officials already know him reasonably well, by seeing them personally and explaining that the document submitted is non-controversial except for paragraph ... ; that the normal wording could not be used because of certain reasons which he then explains verbally.

If it is a short circular he may well be able to return to his office within a matter of minutes with the draft document duly approved; if the company secretary receives a telephone call telling him that he can instruct the printer to go ahead, hours before he expected it, he will realize that the broker is earning his fee.

The broker's job also entails saving the company trouble and expense; for instance—

Example 1. A company had its ordinary capital in £0·20 shares; it decided to make a capitalization issue of 1 for 4 (this naturally entailed a number of fractions); it then proposed to consolidate 5 shares of £0·20 each into 4 shares of £0·25 each (involving a further lot of fractions).

The company was persuaded by the brokers to subdivide the unissued shares of £0·20 each into shares of £0·05 each, to issue one share of £0·05 each, fully paid (25 per cent capitalization) for each £0·20 share held and then to consolidate one £0·05 share with each £0·20 share. Final result, exactly what the company wanted without a single fraction to bedevil the issue.

Example 2. A property company (A) was trying to buy an island site piecemeal—a somewhat lengthy proceeding; in the middle of the negotiations it bought a smaller company (B) which was trying to buy the same site. Company "A" asked company "B" to continue negotiations on its behalf.

The consideration for company "B" was wholly or mainly shares in company "A" identical with "A"'s quoted (unnumbered) shares and it was, therefore, necessary to obtain a quotation for the "vendor" shares.

The Quotations department asked for—

(*a*) A copy of the agreement to be put on view in the solicitor's office
(*b*) An independent valuation

(1) The brokers to company "A" pointed out that, if the agreement were put on view, owners of bits of the island site would flock to see what their neighbours were getting for their properties and might well raise their own selling prices; the brokers made it clear that to do what the Quotations Department asked would be detrimental to the interests of shareholders in company "A" but offered to supply a copy of the agreement to the Quotations Department as a confidential document; this was accepted.

(2) The brokers pointed out that company "A" had a fully qualified surveyor on their staff and that the request for an independent valuation impugned his professional integrity by implication. The Quotations Department agreed to forego the independent valuation and company "A" was thereby saved considerable expense.

Example 3. Company "C" is a very large, internationally known, concern; among its many holdings is a controlling interest (over 60 per cent) in company "D". "D" itself is quite a large company and there is a reasonably free market in its shares. A resolution was to be proposed at the Annual General Meeting of "D"; the Quotations Department insisted on the issue of two-way proxies to shareholders in "D" and this was done.

As the attempt was not made, its result can only be a matter of surmise but it is thought that if the brokers to "D" had pointed out to the Quotations Department (*a*) that, as the controlling company supported the resolution, which only required a simple majority, it was bound to be carried, even if the independent shareholders voted 100 per cent against it and (*b*) that, therefore, the issue of proxies was sheer waste of money, this requirement might have been waived.

Example 4. A company proposed a capitalization issue with "fractions to be ignored"; The Quotations Department immediately asked whether the company's Articles of Association allowed this; they did. The quotation was granted on these terms but the Quotations Department indicated that, if fractional payments had been calculated to exceed about 50p, then objections might have been raised. In excess of this sum, the company might have been required to sell fractions and distribute the proceeds to the shareholder entitled to them.

There are more subtle ways in which the broker to the company can be of service. For example, a company wished to issue shares on which no dividend was to be paid in the immediate future and proposed to designate them "A" ordinary shares. The broker pointed out that in the eyes of the public "A" ordinary shares were non-voting shares and that such a designation would be misleading and could be harmful to the company; the point was taken and "dividend deferred" shares were issued instead.

ADDENDUM

The Finance Act 1972
— Corporate Taxation

THE 1972 Budget will not alter the basic principles of taxation for the year 1972/73 although personal allowances and the starting level for surtax have been changed. It foreshadows, however, fundamental changes starting in the fiscal year 1973/74; one particularly welcome change will be that profits made by companies will not, after suffering Corporation Tax, be fully taxed a second time when distributed as dividends. A further change is that surtax will be abolished and income tax will be graduated.

For purposes of illustration the Government have adopted 50 per cent Corporation Tax, a basic rate of Income Tax of 30 per cent and an Income Tax surcharge of 15 per cent (not on the tax but on the income) on investment income exceeding £2,000. These rates have been used in the examples below. This will be administered on the "imputation" system.

A company will pay interest on loans out of untaxed profits but will deduct income tax at the basic rate and pay this to the Inland Revenue at the time of the interest payment. The remaining profit, after adjustments for capital allowances, foreign tax, etc., will be subject to Corporation Tax.

On paying an ordinary dividend, a further sum, amounting to 3/7ths of the dividend, will be paid to the Inland Revenue as Advance Corporation Tax (ACT); this sum will be credited against the company's liability to Corporation Tax and the credit will be carried forward indefinitely if there is no immediate liability to absorb it, e.g., if the company has made a loss but is paying a dividend out of reserves. The same sum will be "imputed" to the shareholders. For instance, should a company pay an ordinary dividend of £70, it will, at the same time, pay £30 "ACT" to the Inland Revenue. A shareholder receiving £70 ordinary dividend will have £30 "imputed" to him; he will have to declare income of £70 + £30 = £100; should he be liable to income tax at basic rate only, the £30 "imputation" will match his £30 tax liability; however, should his income be such that he is liable to tax at a higher or lower rate or to no tax at all, he will have to pay more or will be able to claim partial or total repayment of the £30.

A preference dividend will be treated slightly differently—30 per cent of the fixed rate will be deducted and paid to the Inland Revenue as ACT; it will also be "imputed" to the shareholder; so the holder of 1,000 7 per cent preference shares of £1 will receive £49 from the company and have £21 (the ACT payment) "imputed" to him; he will have to declare £49 + £21 = £70 income on which £21 has already been credited against his tax liability. The effect of the new system on the company mentioned on pages 66 and 67 is shown below.

This company had £2,237,500 6 per cent Loan Stock outstanding and an issued capital consisting of £1,320,000 7 per cent preference and £3,226,500 ordinary shares; the trading profit was £951,700 after deducting expenses, but before tax.

Loan Interest	Corporation Tax	7% Preference Dividend	12½% Ordinary Dividend	Increase (+) or Decrease (−) or in Carry Forward	Total Earnings
£134,250	£408,725*	£64,680	£282,318	(+) £61,727	£951,700
0–14%	14–57%	57–64%	64–93½%	93½–100%	
£40,275 (deducted and paid to Inland Revenue		£92,400 gross less £27,720 paid to Inland Revenue and credited against Corporation Tax liability	£403,312 gross less £120,994 paid to Inland Revenue and credited against Corporation Tax liability		

* Corporation Tax at 50 per cent on £817,450 (£951,700 less £134,250 gross Loan interest).

The above example ought really to be described as illustrating the effect, not of a 12½ per cent ordinary dividend, but of an ordinary dividend of 7·143 per cent with 5·357 per cent "imputed" to the shareholders, making 12·5 per cent in all.

The following shows the effect of a 12·5 per cent dividend with 5·357 per cent "imputed" to the shareholders; this makes their income 17·857 per cent for tax purposes and their basic tax is 5·357 per cent leaving 12·5 per cent net.

| £134,250 | £408,725 | £64,680 | £403,312 | (−) £59,267 over-allocation |
| 0–14% | 14–57% | 57–64% | 64–106½% | of 6½% |

No system of taxation will ever be perfect; one weakness of the Corporation Tax is that it acts as a direct incentive to bad finance. By making it cheaper for a company to pay interest on a loan than it is to pay the same rate of dividend on a preference or ordinary share, it encourages companies to raise loans, the holders of which are creditors, instead of issuing share capital, the holders of which are members of the company.

Compare the cost to the company of paying 10 per cent interest on £1,000 loan stock and of paying 5 per cent dividend on 1,000 preference shares of £1:

Loan stock

Gross profit		£100
Corporation Tax		nil
		100
To loan holders	£70	
To Inland Revenue	30	—

Preference Capital

Gross profit		£100
Corporation Tax		50
To shareholders	£35	
To Inland Revenue	15	—

Appendix[1]

SCALE OF MINIMUM COMMISSIONS
(Not divisible with an agent) Appendix 39

A. **Securities quoted under the following headings in the Official List—**

British Funds, &c.
Securities issued by the International Bank for Reconstruction and Development
Securities issued by the Inter-American Development Bank
Corporation and County Stocks—Great Britain and Northern Ireland
Public Boards, &c.—Great Britain and Northern Ireland
Commonwealth Government and Provincial Securities
Commonwealth Corporation Stocks

(1) Securities having no final redemption date within ten years

BARGAINS UP TO £50,000 CONSIDERATION
0·5 per cent on the first   £2,000 consideration
0·2 per cent on the next £12,000 consideration
0·1 per cent on the next £36,000 consideration.

BARGAINS OVER £50,000 CONSIDERATION
A flat rate of 0·14 per cent up to £4m. consideration
0·07 per cent on the excess, subject to Rule 208.

(2) New Issues referred to in Rule 209

BARGAINS UP TO £50,000 CONSIDERATION
0·5 per cent   on the first   £2,000 consideration
0·1 per cent   on the next   £2,000 consideration
0·05 per cent on the next £46,000 consideration.

BARGAINS OVER £50,000 CONSIDERATION
A flat rate of 0·07 per cent on consideration.

(3) Securities having ten years or less to final redemption

BARGAINS UP TO £50,000 CONSIDERATION
0·5 per cent   on the first   £2,000 consideration
0·1 per cent   on the next   £2,000 consideration
0·05 per cent on the next £46,000 consideration.

BARGAINS OVER £50,000 CONSIDERATION
A flat rate of 0·07 per cent up to £4m. consideration
0·035 per cent on the excess, subject to Rule 208.

(4) Securities having five years or less to final redemption and not in default
At discretion.

[1] From January 1973 some further concessions were allowed in both Appendix 39 and 41 to large transactions in excess of £50,000.

B. **Debentures, bonds, &c.**

Debentures and Bonds and any other securities representing loans (Debenture Stocks, Loan Stocks, Notes, Annuities, etc.) other than those included in Section A above.

(1) Registered*

0·75 per cent   on the first   £5,000 consideration
0·375 per cent on the next   £15,000 consideration
Nil   on the next   £5,000 consideration
0·375 per cent on the next £475,000 consideration
0·3 per cent   on the excess.

* Including New Issues passing by delivery in scrip form or by letters of renunciation.

(2) Bearer

0·5 per cent   on the first   £5,000 consideration
0·25 per cent on the next £15,000 consideration
Nil   on the next   £5,000 consideration
0·25 per cent on the excess.

(3) Euro-Currency Bonds, i.e. Fixed Income Securities (excluding Preferred Stock and Preference Share Capital) issued after 1st January, 1963, on which capital moneys are payable in a foreign currency listed below and, except in the case of Japanese issues, the interest on which is payable without deduction of tax at source

U.S. dollars (external)	French Francs
Dutch Florins	Luxembourg Francs
Lire	Belgian Francs
Deutsche Mark	Swiss Francs
Sterling/Deutsche Mark	E.U.A. (European Units of Account)

At discretion.

(4) Other Loans quoted in London expressed or optionally payable in a foreign currency other than that of a Scheduled Territory
0·25 per cent on consideration.

C. **Stocks and Shares**

Stocks and Shares Registered or Bearer (other than those in Sections A, B or D) whether partly or fully paid

1·25 per cent   on the first   £5,000 consideration
0·625 per cent on the next £15,000 consideration
Nil   on the next   £5,000 consideration
0·625 per cent on the next £50,000 consideration
0·5 per cent   on the excess.

D. **American and Canadian Shares**

Shares of Companies incorporated in the United States of America or Canada (whether dealt in in London on a Dollar or Sterling basis), with the exception of Shares which are deliverable by Transfer

0·75 per cent   on the first   £5,000 consideration
0·375 per cent on the next   £15,000 consideration

Nil   on the next £5,000 consideration
0·375 per cent on the excess.
See Rule 204 (2)—Commission on American and Canadian
            Securities.

E.   **Short-Dated Securities**
Securities having five years or less to final redemption and not in
default
    At discretion.

F.   **Unquoted units of Unit Trust**
    At discretion.

G.   **Options**
"Givers" of option money for more than one Account
    As laid down in Rule 210 (1).
"Takers" of option money for more than one Account
    As laid down in Rule 210 (5).
Options for one Account or less
    At discretion.

H.   **Small Bargains**

	Securities in SECTION A	Securities in all other Sections
The minimum commission to be charged shall be	£2	£4
except in the case of		
(1) Transactions on which the Commission may be	at discretion	at discretion
(2) Transactions amounting to less than £100 in value on which commission must be charge at not less than	£1	£2
(3) Transactions amounting to less than £10 in value on which commission may be	at discretion	at discretion

I.   **Valuations**
(1) Probate Valuations
    Under £5,000
        At discretion.
    £5,000 or over
        0·05 per cent   on the Probate value up to £100,000
        0·0125 per cent on the balance, subject to a minimum charge
             50*p*. per item.
    Subject to Rule 200 (4).

(2) All other valuations
    At discretion.

SCALE OF MINIMUM COMMISSIONS
(when divisible with an agent) Appendix 41

A. **Securities quoted under the following headings in the Official List—**

British Funds, &c.
Securities issued by the International Bank for Reconstruction and Development
Securities issued by the Inter-American Development Bank
Corporation and County Stocks—Great Britain and Northern Ireland
Public Boards, &c.—Great Britain and Northern Ireland
Commonwealth Government and Provincial Securities
Commonwealth Corporation Stocks

(1) Securities having no final redemption date within ten years
BARGAINS UP TO £50,000 CONSIDERATION
0·625 per cent on the first   £2,000 consideration
0·25 per cent on the next £12,000 consideration
0·125 per cent on the next £36,000 consideration.

BARGAINS OVER £50,000 CONSIDERATION
A flat rate of 0·175 per cent up to £4m. consideration
0·08 per cent on the excess, subject to Rule 208.

(2) New Issues referred to in Rule 209
BARGAINS UP TO £50,000 CONSIDERATION
0·625 per cent on the first   £2,000 consideration
0·125 per cent on the next   £2,000 consideration
0·0625 per cent on the next £46,000 consideration.

BARGAINS OVER £50,000 CONSIDERATION
A flat rate of 0·0875 per cent on consideration.

(3) Securities having ten years or less to final redemption
BARGAINS UP TO £50,000 CONSIDERATION
0·625 per cent on the first   £2,000 consideration
0·125 per cent on the next   £2,000 consideration
0·0625 per cent on the next £46,000 consideration.

BARGAINS OVER £50,000 CONSIDERATION
A flat rate of 0·0875 per cent up to £4m. consideration
0·04 per cent on the excess, subject to Rule 208.

(4) Securities having five years or less to final redemption and not in default
At discretion.

B. **Debentures, Bonds, &c.**
Debentures and Bonds and any other securities representing loans (Debenture Stocks, Loan Stocks, Notes, Annuities, &c.) other than those included in Section A above—

(1) Registered
0·75 per cent on the first   £20,000 consideration
0·45 per cent on the next £480,000 consideration
0·35 per cent on the excess.

(2) Bearer
> 0·5 per cent on the first £20,000 consideration
> 0·3 per cent on the excess.

(3) Euro-Currency Bonds, i.e. Fixed Income Securities (excluding Preferred Stock and Preference Share Capital) issued after 1st January, 1963, on which capital moneys are payable in a foreign currency listed below and, except in the case of Japanese issues, the interest on which is payable without deduction of tax at source

U.S. dollars (external)	French Francs
Dutch Florins	Luxembourg Francs
Lire	Belgian Francs
Deutsche Mark	Swiss Francs
Sterling/Deutsche Mark	E.U.A. (European Units of Account)

> At discretion.

(4) Other Loans quoted in London expressed or optionally payable in a foreign currency other than that of a Scheduled Territory
> 0·3 per cent on consideration.

C.   Stocks and Shares

Stocks and Shares, Registered or Bearer (other than those in Sections A, B or D) whether partly or fully paid
> 1·25 per cent on the first £20,000 consideration
> 0·75 per cent on the next £55,000 consideration
> 0·6 per cent   on the excess.

D.   American and Canadian Shares

Shares of Companies incorporated in the United States of America or Canada (whether dealt in in London on a Dollar or Sterling basis), with the exception of Shares which are deliverable by Transfer
> 0·75 per cent on the first £20,000 consideration
> 0·45 per cent on the excess.

> See Rule 204 (2)—Commission on American and Canadian Securities.

E.   Short-Dated Securities

Securities having five years or less to final redemption and not in default
> At discretion.

F.   Unquoted units of Unit Trusts

> At discretion.

G.   Options

"Givers" of option money for more than one Account
> As laid down in Rule 210 (1).

"Takers" of option money for more than one Account
> As laid down in Rule 210 (5).

Options for one Account or less
> At discretion.

H.   **Small Bargains**

	Securities in SECTION A	Securities in all other Sections
The minimum commission to be charged shall be except in the case of	£2	£4
(1) Transactions on which the Commission may be	at discretion	at discretion
(2) Transactions amounting to less than £100 in value on which commission must be charged at not less than	£1	£2
(3) Transactions amounting to less than £10 in value on which commission may be	at discretion	at discretion

STAMP DUTIES ON TRANSFERS

Consideration not exceeding £											Amount £
5	.	.	.	.	.	.	.	.	.	.	0·05
10	.	.	.	.	.	.	.	.	.	.	0·10
20	.	.	.	.	.	.	.	.	.	.	0·20
30	.	.	.	.	.	.	.	.	.	.	0·30
40	.	.	.	.	.	.	.	.	.	.	0·40
50	.	.	.	.	.	.	.	.	.	.	0·50
60	.	.	.	.	.	.	.	.	.	.	0·60
70	.	.	.	.	.	.	.	.	.	.	0·70
80	.	.	.	.	.	.	.	.	.	.	0·80
90	.	.	.	.	.	.	.	.	.	.	0·90
100	.	.	.	.	.	.	.	.	.	.	1·00
120	.	.	.	.	.	.	.	.	.	.	1·20
140	.	.	.	.	.	.	.	.	.	.	1·40
160	.	.	.	.	.	.	.	.	.	.	1·60
180	.	.	.	.	.	.	.	.	.	.	1·80
200	.	.	.	.	.	.	.	.	.	.	2·00
220	.	.	.	.	.	.	.	.	.	.	2·20
240	.	.	.	.	.	.	.	.	.	.	2·40
260	.	.	.	.	.	.	.	.	.	.	2·60
280	.	.	.	.	.	.	.	.	.	.	2·80
300	.	.	.	.	.	.	.	.	.	.	3·00
350	.	.	.	.	.	.	.	.	.	.	3·50
400	.	.	.	.	.	.	.	.	.	.	4·00

and so on at the rate of £0·50 for every further £50 or fractional part of £50.

Contract Stamp Duty

Where the value of the stock or marketable security—is £100 or less   .   nil

Exceeds £100 and does not exceed £500 .   .   .   .   .   . £0·10

  ,,   £500   ,,   ,, £1500 .   .   .   .   .   . £0·30

  ,,   £1500 .   .   .   . £0·60

Note. Contract stamp is payable on any bargain, irrespective of the nature of the security.

No transfer stamp is payable on British Funds or Dominion Stocks—it is now payable on Southern Rhodesian stocks, however—or on Corporation or County stocks (Great Britain and Northern Ireland). In the case of Public Boards, e.g. Port of London Authority, some stocks are subject to transfer stamp duty while others are not (for details see the Stock Exchange Official Intelligence).

Glossary

ACCOUNT DAY. The day on which all bargains done for the account are settled; the Account Day is always a Tuesday.

ACCRUED INTEREST. British Government and British Municipal Loans with less than five years to final redemption date are dealt in at prices which refer to the stock alone; interest for the number of days since the last interest payment is calculated separately and added or, if the price has recently been made "ex dividend", interest for the number of days to the next interest payment date is subtracted. The accrued interest without deduction of tax is shown separately on the contract and is regarded by the Inland Revenue as an adjustment to the price and not as income.

ACTUAL. Dividends are usually declared as so and so much per cent (actual) but are sometimes declared as "at the rate of so and so much per cent per annum for such and such a period"; a dividend at the rate of 5 per cent per annum for six months is equivalent to $2\frac{1}{2}$ per cent actual.

ALLOTMENT LETTER. Letter from a company informing the person to whom it is addressed that he has been allotted so many new shares. Some allotment letters are non-renounceable and the shares can only be transferred by deed. In most cases they are renounceable in which case there is a "Renunciation Form" on the back; when this has been signed by the Allottee the shares will be transferred without expense to the person whose name and address are placed in the appropriate space on the form, provided the letter is registered with the company before the final renunciation date. The allotment letter also embodies a form of receipt to be signed on behalf of the company when the appropriate payment is made. In the case of a capitalization issue the shares are allotted fully paid; there is, therefore, no payment to be made and no form of receipt. Capitalization issues are now usually but not always made in the form of renounceable certificates.

AMERICAN FORM. American and Canadian shares are dealt in in the form of registered certificates endorsed in blank. In order to be "good delivery" in London, certificates must represent not more than 100 shares of up to $5 each, 50 shares of up to $25 each, 20 shares of up to $50 each or 10 shares of any higher denomination or shares of no par value.

AND OVER, AND UNDER. One sixty-fourth of a pound. "An eighth to three-sixteenths and over" means "$\frac{1}{8}$ to $\frac{3}{16}$ plus $\frac{1}{64}$"; "an eighth to a quarter and under" means "$\frac{1}{8}$ to $\frac{7}{32}$ plus $\frac{1}{64}$." Not to be confused with "over" and "under," both of which mean a thirty-second of a pound. "An

eighth to over" means "$\frac{1}{8}$ to $\frac{5}{32}$"; "under to a quarter" means "$\frac{7}{32}$ to $\frac{1}{4}$."
A thirty-second of a pound is $3\frac{1}{2}$p. and a sixty-fourth is $1\frac{1}{2}$p. It is usual
to write $\frac{3}{16} + \frac{1}{64}$ rather than $\frac{13}{64}$.

ANOMALY. From time to time a stock or share is overlooked or is unduly
depressed by the liquidation of a deceased estate or the price is forced
up by a bear squeeze so that the yield is out of line with those of comparable securities. Astute operators take advantage of this as soon as
they notice it and the anomaly is soon corrected.

APPLICATION FORM. When securities are offered for public subscription,
application has to be made on special forms obtainable from the issuing
house or from the company's brokers or bankers either direct or through
the client's own broker or banker. The forms are also printed at the
bottom of the prospectus advertised in the daily press. In many cases a
small commission is payable by the issuing house in respect of the number of shares allotted (not the number applied for) to the banker or
broker whose rubber stamp appears on the form.

AT BEST. Abbreviation for "at the lowest possible price," in the case of a
buying order, and "at the highest possible price," in the case of a
selling order.

BACK OR BACKWARDATION. Fee paid by a bear on borrowing stock or shares
to deliver against his sale. Also, market term for the situation when one
jobber's offer price is lower than another jobber's bid price. No broker
may deal without disclosing that a "back" exists.

BAD DELIVERY. Bonds which have been damaged or have not got the proper
coupons attached; American or Canadian shares registered in other
than Recognized Marking Names unless sold as "in other names."
Shares with distinctive numbers other than those in which permission to
deal has been granted. Registered securities in respect of which the
transfer is not in order, e.g. signature of transferor does not agree with
name on certificate. The buyer is entitled to refuse to accept and pay
for securities which are not good delivery.

BAD NAMES. *See* OTHER NAMES.

BEAR. One who has sold stock or shares which he does not possess, in the
hope of buying it (them) back at a lower price.

BEAR SQUEEZE. *See* SQUEEZE.

BIG FIGURE. *See* FIGURE.

BARGAIN. Any transaction in the Stock Exchange; also cheap stock.

BLUE CHIPS. The shares with the highest status as investments, particularly
in the industrial markets. The first "blue chips" that come to mind are
Bats, Courtaulds, Imperial Chemicals, Imp. Tobacco, Unilever, Tur-
ner & Newall, etc.

BONUS. *See* CAPITAL BONUS and CASH BONUS.

BUCKET SHOP. A firm outside the Stock Exchange which deals in stocks and
shares; the term rather suggests a fraudulent concern, but there are
reputable outside houses. Some outside houses are limited companies.
The Bucket Shop seems to have disappeared as the result of the Prevention of Fraud Act.

BUDGET DAY PRICE. The middle price in the Official Quotation in the

Stock Exchange Official List of 6th April, 1965, or the mean of the marks recorded in the Official List of 6th April, 1965, referring to business done on that day, and the marks recorded in the following day's Official List as referring to transactions on 6th April, whichever is higher. Marks at special prices are excluded. This price is required for the computation of capital gains tax.

BULL. One who has bought stock for a quick profit; the term "bull" implies that the speculator does not intend to pay for the stock, but that he will take a profit, cut a loss, or contango the stock.

CALL. Demand by a company for payment by the shareholder of part or all of the unpaid portion of a partly-paid share.

CALL. Right to buy stock or shares at the agreed option price.

CALL. Exercise an option to buy stock or shares at the option price.

CAPITAL BONUS. *See* CAPITALIZATION ISSUE.

CAPITALIZATION ISSUE. Issue of new shares made fully paid by the capitalization of reserves and made free of charge to ordinary shareholders in proportion to their existing holdings. Fractions of shares are sometimes disregarded, but more often they are aggregated and sold, after which a cash payment in respect of fractions is made to each shareholder entitled to it; such an issue is often loosely termed a Capital Bonus or Scrip Bonus, but these terms are misleading as the reserves thus capitalized belonged to the ordinary shareholders in any case.

CARRY OVER. *See* CONTANGO.

CASH AND NEW. The term used when shares bought during the account are sold free of commission to close and are immediately re-purchased for the new account. Normally, a premium is payable when stock is bought for the new account (about 2p in the pound) but at the jobber's discretion this is reduced for dealing "cash and new." This operation is much the same as carrying over stock as it postpones payment of the shares from the coming account day to the next; in effect, the jobber is lending the money for the duration of the account and is entitled to be paid for this service. This form of business is generally discouraged.

CASH BONUS. Extra dividend; the term implies that the bonus is paid in respect of an exceptionally profitable year. A cash bonus is sometimes paid out of capital profits.

CASH FLOW. Cash earned by a company but not distributed; whether it is used to increase the carry-forward or allocated to depreciation or reserve is immaterial. Briefly, it is the difference between the amount of net earnings, after tax, and the amount, after tax, distributed as dividend. A large cash flow implies the ability to finance new developments without raising fresh money.

C.D. Abbreviation for cum dividend: usually printed c.d.

CHOICE. When one jobber is offering stock at the same price as another jobber is bidding. A broker should not deal without disclosing that he has his choice.

CLIENT. People who deal through stockbrokers are known as clients.

CLOSE. $\frac{1}{64}$ of £1 when the price is quoted in pounds. Before decimalization $\frac{1}{64}$ of a pound was 3¾d., or in decimals, approximately 1½p. Thus, if the "figure" (q.v.) was 2, then "close to the figure" means that the jobber will buy at 1 $\frac{31}{32}$ + $\frac{1}{64}$ i.e. 39/8$\frac{1}{4}$d or, in decimals, about £1·98$\frac{1}{2}$. When prices were quoted in shillings and pence "close" meant $\frac{3}{4}$d; thus "10/4$\frac{1}{2}$d close to close" meant that the jobber would buy at 10/3$\frac{3}{4}$d or sell at 10/5$\frac{1}{4}$d. At the time of writing it seems that the latter use will disappear, and the former will likely be confined to the "gilt edged" market.

CONCESSIONS. The main concessions in the commission rules are the following—

Free to Close. If the same stocks or shares are bought and sold during the same "account," the closing bargain may be done free of commission. Where bargains are done for cash this concession covers a period of 28 days in the case of "gilt-edged" and a period of 14 days in the case of Renunciation Letters.

Reduced Commission Re-investment. This concession was rescinded with effect from June 1966.

£5,000 *Rule.* If the consideration exceeded £5,000, full commission had to be charged on £5,000 and half commission on the balance of the consideration. The concession was not allowed if the commission was shared with an agent. There were other concessions applying to "gilt edged" dealings and to transactions over £25,000. The effect of this concession has now been embodied in the commission scale and accounts for the curious feature that, when a large order is executed in an equity, 1·25 per cent is charged on the first £5,000 consideration, 0·625 per cent on the next £15,000, nil on the next £5,000, 0·625 per cent on the next £50,000 and 0·5 per cent on the excess. Commission on this scale may not be shared with an agent; there is now a separate commission scale when it is to be shared with an agent.

Any concession is theoretically permissive and not mandatory; i.e. it is a case of "may" and not of "must," since the Rules of the Stock Exchange say that brokers "may make this concession if they consider that the amount of business done by the client concerned justifies the concession."

In practice, any concession is always made.

Two concessions exclude each other so that clients cannot receive the benefits of both. (There are other concessions applying to "gilt-edged" dealings.)

CONSIDERATION. The money paid for an amount of stock or a number of shares exclusive of commission, transfer expenses, etc.

CONTANGO. Rate of interest paid by a bull on money borrowed with which to pay for stock which he has bought; the money is borrowed from one account day to the next account day, and the bull is said to "contango" the stock or to "carry it over."

CONTANGO DAY. Contangos are now arranged on the last dealing day of the account; formerly Contango Day was the first day.

COVER. The ratio of the profit, after tax and prior charges, to the ordinary dividend; if the dividend was declared gross it was the practice to gross up the amount available for distribution as dividend to get "the earnings". Thus when tax was £0·41$\frac{1}{4}$ in £1, if £23,500 was available for distribution to the ordinary shareholders and £11,750 (£20,000 less tax at £0·41¼) was paid by way of a 10 per cent gross dividend, the earnings were said to be 20 per cent. If the £1 shares stood at £2·00, the dividend yield was 5 per cent, the earnings yield was 10 per cent and the dividend was covered twice.

CUM DIVIDEND. A stock or share is said to be cum dividend when the price includes the dividend or interest which is shortly to be paid. Similarly "cum capitalization" and "cum rights."

DEBENTURE and DEBENTURE STOCK. Security issued by a company under a trust deed against a loan; the trustees for the debenture issue can, if necessary, put the company into liquidation to protect the interests of the debenture holders. Debenture stock can be transferable in any amount (usually in multiples of £1) and a new certificate is issued to each new holder. Debentures which were formerly in bearer form are indivisible and usually for £100 or £500; they are now transferable by deed but the name of the holder is written in on the back after crossing out the name of the previous holder by an official of the company.

DECLARATION. Options done for the Account may be declared by the buyer of the Option not later than 2.45 p.m. on the penultimate Dealing Day (Thursday) in any Account during the currency of the Option. (The buyer of the Option "declares" that he will call (or put) the shares or that he will abandon the Option.) When, on account of a Bank Holiday, dealing for the new account starts on a Friday or on the Thursday before Good Friday, the Declaration Day is put back to the Wednesday or Tuesday.

DEED OF TRANSFER. Legal instrument by which stock or shares are transferred from one holder to another; the term is usually abbreviated to "transfer."

DISCOUNT. New issues may be dealt in at PAR (the issue price) at so and so much premium over the issue price, or at so and so much discount on the issue price while they are partly paid, but they may also be dealt in at prices which include the amount paid, e.g. a share issued at £1·00, 50p paid, might be dealt in at 2½p discount or at £0·47½ which is the same thing. It must be remembered that the jobber making a new penny price on this example would make 3p to 2p discount, both 50p paid, which is the same price as £0·47 to £0·48. Rights issues, nil paid, are dealt in at so and so much premium; there is no point in dealing in them at a discount which would, in effect, amount to paying the buyer to take them away when it would be cheaper to tear up the provisional allotment letter. Acceptance of the shares which is done by paying the first call binds the acceptor to pay the remaining call or calls at the due date(s).

DIVIDEND. Distribution of profit to shareholders.

DIVIDEND MANDATE or DIVIDEND REQUEST FORM. Printed form to be completed by the shareholder requesting the company to pay all dividends on shares registered in his name to his bank, whose receipt shall be the company's full and sufficient discharge. Also used in respect of payment of interest on Government loans and on company debentures.

EARNINGS. *See* COVER and PRICE/EARNINGS RATIO.

Either side. Short for one thirty-second of £1, or $3\frac{1}{8}$p, either side of the price mentioned; "either side of three-quarters" or "three-quarters, either side" means that the jobber will buy at $\frac{1}{32}$ under $\frac{3}{4}$ (or $\frac{23}{32}$) or sell at $\frac{1}{32}$ over $\frac{3}{4}$ (or $\frac{25}{32}$).

Eurodollars. Dollars received by non-United States citizens in payment for goods, services, the building of factories or the acquisition of businesses, which then remain outside the United States. The recipients either retain the dollars, lend or sell them to other non-United States citizens or organizations as "Eurodollars."

Ex Cap'n. When a company issues new shares fully paid by capitalization of reserves or share premium account the price is made "ex capitalization" on the day on which the new shares are issued, and is adjusted accordingly (*see* Ex Rights).

Ex Dividend. A stock or share is quoted ex dividend when the amount (less tax) of the dividend or interest recently paid or shortly to be paid, has been deducted from the price. When a stock is dealt in "ex dividend" the seller retains the dividend. The term also does duty for "ex interest" which has fallen into desuetude.

Ex Rights. When new shares are issued to shareholders in proportion to their existing holdings, at a price below the current market price, the right to subscribe is valued by the Stock Exchange authorities and when the new shares are issued the old shares are made "ex rights," the price being adjusted by deducting the value of the rights. (*See* page 78.)

Figure. When quoting the prices of active stocks, it is assumed that the big figure is known. Thus a share standing at $3\frac{5}{8}$ may be quoted as "nine eleven," i.e. $3\frac{9}{16}$—$3\frac{11}{16}$, and a share standing at 4 may be quoted as "either side of the figure," i.e. $3\frac{31}{32}$—$4\frac{1}{32}$. A stock standing at $99\frac{1}{2}$ may be quoted as "nine and three-eighths five-eighths" i.e. $99\frac{3}{8}$—$99\frac{5}{8}$, or possibly simply as "three-eighths five-eighths."

Final Dividend. When a company has paid one or more "interim dividends" (q.v.), the dividend declared at the annual general meeting is known as the "final dividend," i.e. the final dividend for the financial year, the accounts in respect of which have been considered at the meeting.

Flat Yield. Yield calculated on the price of the stock without allowance for profit or loss on redemption. Also known as "Running Yield."

Franked Income. Income, e.g. in the hands of an investment trust, that has already suffered corporation tax; corporation tax is not payable a second time on franked income. The term formerly applied to profits tax.

Free. Free of transfer expenses; when small or odd lots of shares were sold, it was usual to sell them "free," the seller instead of the buyer paying the transfer expenses. Such bargains are done "for cash." Owing to the inconvenience of having to deal with "cash" bargains in mechanized offices, it is now more usual to accept a lower price for small lots and sell them "for the account." The net result is much the same.

Free to Close. *See* under "Concessions—*Free to Close*."

FUNDS, THE. United Kingdom Government stocks are sometimes known collectively as "The Funds."

GILT-EDGED. United Kingdom Government and Government Guaranteed stocks, Dominion and Municipal stocks, etc.

GIVE ON. This is short for "give a rate on" when a bull carries stock over. *See* CONTANGO.

GOOD DELIVERY. Bonds which are undamaged, not drawn for redemption (unless so specified at the time the bargain was done) and with the proper coupons attached. American and Canadian shares, properly stamped, in recognized marking names (q.v.) unless otherwise specified at the time the bargain was done. Registered securities in proper order.

GOOD NAMES. *See* MARKING NAMES.

INCOME BONDS and INCOME DEBENTURES. Bonds and debentures or debenture stock, the interest on which is only payable out of profits; they originate from an arrangement with the company's creditors.

INCOME TAX is deducted at source from dividend and interest payments (registered War Loan $3\frac{1}{2}$ per cent is the only important exception); a so-called tax-free dividend is really a correspondingly larger dividend less tax. Vouchers stating so and so much tax has been deducted and has been, or will be, paid to the Inland Revenue, accompany all dividend and interest payments. These vouchers have to be produced in support of claims for refund of income tax overpaid.

INDEMNITY, LETTER OF. When a stock or share certificate has been lost or destroyed, the company concerned will usually issue a duplicate on receiving a letter signed by the shareholder (over a sixpenny stamp) explaining the circumstances and undertaking to indemnify the company for any loss incurred as the result of the issue of a duplicate certificate (or allotment letter). Many companies insist on the client's bank joining in the indemnity and this may necessitate the manager of the branch where the client keeps his account applying to Head Office for the authority to sign the indemnity on behalf of the bank. Bearer securities are never seen by the client, since they have to be kept by an "authorized depositary" but it should be noted that, if bearer securities are lost, stolen or destroyed, they are virtually irreplaceable.

INSCRIBED STOCK. Stock which used to be transferred from seller to buyer by the transferor or his attorney "signing off" the stock at the Bank of England (or wherever the books of the particular stock are kept).

No stock certificate was issued to the buyer. Such stocks are now transferred by deed and a certificate is issued to the buyer. A holder of inscribed stock can obtain a certificate on request, but there is no need for him to do so, as transfers will be certified by the Bank of England for delivery against a sale. Some stocks are still described as "Inscribed Stock" but, as they are transferred by deed, they are really registered stocks.

INTERIM DIVIDEND. As it is inconvenient for shareholders to receive dividends only once a year, many companies pay one or more "interim dividends" on account of the current year. The payment of an interim dividend does not necessarily mean that a final dividend (q.v.) will be declared, nor does it give any indication of the amount of the final dividend. The directors have power to declare and pay an interim dividend but the final dividend, in the case of most companies, has to be sanctioned by the shareholders in general meeting before it may be paid. Some companies pay a small interim and a large final dividend; some make the interim and final dividends approximately equal.

ISSUE ON BONUS TERMS. Issue of new shares to shareholders at a price below the current price of the old shares.

JOBBER. One who makes a market in a stock or share, and who only deals with other members of the Stock Exchange.

LETTER OF—ALLOTMENT (q.v.) INDEMNITY (q.v.) PROVISIONAL ALLOTMENT (q.v.) REGRET (q.v.) RENUNCIATION (q.v.) REQUEST (q.v.)

LIMIT. An order to buy at below, or to sell at above, the current price at a limit fixed by the client; when giving a limit the client should say for how long it is to be kept in force, e.g. good for the (current) account, good till cancelled.

MARK OR MARKING. A price given in the newspapers under the heading "record of business done" at which business has been done on the previous day. (The Saturday issues of financial dailies record the last bargain during the week and the date on which it was done, if no mark was recorded on the Friday.) The number of marks gives a rough guide to the activity of the stock but it must be remembered that when a number of bargains are done at the same price they are not all recorded individually. The newspapers obtain the markings from the Official List published by the Stock Exchange Council every afternoon.

MARKET NAMES. Synonymous with Marking Names.

MARKING NAMES. American and Canadian shares are dealt in in the form of share certificates endorsed in blank. These are not good delivery (unless otherwise stipulated at the time the bargain was done) unless they are registered in the names of certain finance houses, jobbers or brokers recorded in a list of "Recognized Marking Names" kept by the Stock Exchange authorities. These firms undertake to receive the dividends from the companies and to pay them to the owners of the shares when the share certificates are presented to be "marked for dividend." (*See* page 37.)

MIDDLE PRICE. The price half-way between the two prices quoted in the Stock Exchange Official List; it is used for making valuations for most purposes except for Probate q.v. Most newspapers only publish the middle prices, but those are the latest available and may differ from those in the Official List.

NAME. (The proper term is "ticket") issued by the buyer's broker giving the buyer's name and the consideration required by the seller's broker to enable him to prepare the transfer. The buyer's name no longer appears on the ticket, except in the case of securities to which the Stock Transfer Act, 1963, does not apply.

N.B.I. Not to "buy in."

NOMINAL VALUE is the par or face value of a share or bond.

NOMINAL PRICE. *See* QUOTATION.

N.P.V. No par value. *See* pages 9, 39.

NOT TO PRESS or N.T.P. When a jobber has no stock, he will sometimes sell on the understanding that the buyer will not press for delivery. N.B.I. is a more precise definition of the same gentleman's agreement.

OFFICIAL LIST. *See* STOCK EXCHANGE OFFICIAL LIST.

ON TAP. *See* TAP LOANS.

OTHER NAMES. American and Canadian shares registered in names other than "Recognized Marking Names" are not good delivery against a sale unless "Other Names" was specified at the time the bargain was done. Shares in "Other Names" normally command a lower price than shares in Recognized Marking or "good" names. "Other Names" are also referred to as "bad" names or "private" names.

OUTSIDE HOUSE. Firm whose partners are not members of the Stock Exchange, which deals in stocks and shares. Some outside houses are limited companies. *See* BUCKET SHOP.

OVER means $\frac{1}{32}$ of £1, or $3\frac{1}{8}$p. Thus "half to over" means £0·50 to £0·53$\frac{1}{8}$; "over the three" means $\frac{1}{32}$ over three-sixteenths, i.e. $\frac{7}{32}$ or £0·21$\frac{7}{8}$, and so on. "Over the three" must be carefully distinguished from "three-sixteenths and over" which means $\frac{1}{64}$ over three-sixteenths, i.e. $\frac{3}{16} + \frac{1}{64}$.

PAR is 100 in the case of stock, and the face or nominal value in the case of shares, with the following important exception. In the case of partly-paid new issues, both of stocks and of shares, PAR is the issue price.

PARITY. The sterling equivalent (without the dollar premium) of the American or Canadian price at the current rate of exchange. It is worth noting that American and Canadian prices are "bid" prices, i.e. prices at which the shares in question can be sold, whereas in London, when only a single price is given, it is understood to be the middle price.

PASSED. When a company decides not to declare a dividend, the dividend is said to be passed.

PAY DAY. Account day; the day on which all bargains done for the account are settled.

PINK FORM. *See* PREFERENTIAL FORM.

PREFERENTIAL FORM. When companies offer new shares for public subscription they usually give preferential treatment to applications from their own shareholders; for this purpose they issue preferential application forms which are readily distinguishable by their colour, usually pink; they are often called "Pink Forms."

PRELIMINARY DAY. First day of dealings for an account. Also the first day on which bought tickets are prepared.

PREMIUM. New issues are dealt in at PAR (the issue price), at so and so much premium over the issue price, or at so and so much discount on the issue price, until they are fully paid.

PRICE/EARNINGS RATIO (P/E). An American yardstick, now widely used over here, is the ratio of the price to the distributable earnings. A share with earnings available for distribution to ordinary shareholders, after corporation tax and prior charges of 5p per share, priced in the market at £0·60 has a P/E of 12. This ratio is virtually the reciprocal of the earnings yield.

PRIOR CHARGES. Those securities on which the interest (on debentures and loans) and dividends (on preference shares) must be paid before any dividend may be paid to ordinary shareholders. In a winding-up the holders of debentures and loans (creditors of the company) and preference shares (members of the company) rank for payment before the holders of ordinary and deferred shares.

PRIORITY PERCENTAGES. *See* page 65.

PRIVATE NAMES. *See* OTHER NAMES.

PROBATE PRICE. One-quarter of the way up from the lower to the higher price in the official quotation, e.g. quotation £1·000–£1·050; probate price £1·0125.

PROVISIONAL ALLOTMENT LETTER. Offers of new shares in proportion to their existing holdings are made to shareholders by provisional letters of allotment. *See* page 75.

PUT. Right to sell stock or shares at the agreed option price.

PUT. Exercise an option to sell stock or shares at the option price.

PUT THROUGH. When buying and selling orders in the same security reach a broker, he "puts the shares through" a jobber for a small turn, i.e., he sells them to the jobber and buys them back at a slightly higher price; in return for this the jobber guarantees the prices are fair to both buyer and seller. The jobber is entitled to reduce one side of the bargain to cover his bear position or to reduce his bull position. In the case of a very large put through, the jobber may be asked to share his turn with other jobbers who deal in the shares.

QUOTATION is a double price, the lower being the price at which the stock can be sold, and the higher, the price at which it can be bought. Nominal Quotation—A double price indicating the basis of negotiation, when there is no free market in the stock.

RECOGNIZED MARKING NAMES. *See* MARKING NAMES.

REDEMPTION. Repayment of a loan.

REGRET, LETTER OF. Letter sent to unsuccessful applicant informing him that no new shares (stock) have been allotted to him.

RENUNCIATION, LETTER OF. Allotment letter duly renounced by the original allottee.

REQUEST, LETTER OF. Letter to a company from an executor asking that stock or shares registered in his name as executor of the deceased should be registered in his own name as a private individual.

RIGHTS. Fresh capital is often raised by offering new shares to shareholders in proportion to their holdings. Such an issue is said to be made by way of "rights" and when the provisional allotment letters have been issued the value of the rights is deducted from the price of the old shares, which are then quoted "ex rights." (*See* page 78.) Similarly with capitalization issues when the new shares are issued fully paid.

RUNNING YIELD. *See* FLAT YIELD.

SCRIP BONUS. *See* CAPITALIZATION ISSUE.

SHORTS. British Government and British Municipal loans with less than five years to go to the final redemption date; these are dealt in "plus accrued interest" reckoned in days.

SOUTH AFRICAN GOVERNMENT STAMP. One rand per R100 (£58·33) or part of R100 consideration must be charged to the buyer of shares in companies registered in South Africa.

SQUEEZE, BEAR. When bears are unable to borrow stock to deliver against their sales and the price is forced up against them, they are said to be "squeezed," since they must buy back the shares they have sold as they cannot deliver them.

STAG. One who applies for a new issue in the hope of being able to sell what is allotted to him at a premium at once.

STALE BULL. One who has bought stock in anticipation of a quick rise which has failed to materialize.

STAMP DUTY. Stamp duties payable on deeds of transfer and on contract notes are set out on another page.

There are certain exceptions in the case of transfers.

Transfers may be made on a fifty new pence stamp in a number of cases, some of which are—

Securities taken up by a jobber in the ordinary course of business; the jobber is liable for the balance of the full duty if the securities are not delivered out of his name within two months.

Where there is no change of beneficial ownership, e.g., from the beneficial owner to a bank nominee company to be held on his behalf.

From an executor to a residuary legatee.

From an executor to a beneficiary in settlement of a specific bequest.

(It should be noted that, if an executor delivers securities to a beneficiary in lieu of cash, full stamp duty is payable.)

When a consideration is paid by the seller to the buyer (e.g. a seller pays a buyer to relieve him of the potential liability on a partly-paid share) the transfer is made for a nominal consideration of 25p and the stamp duty is 50p.

Gifts *inter vivos* attract the full stamp duty that would have been payable on a consideration calculated on the middle price.

Stamp duty is payable, once and for always, on warrants to bearer, in respect of shares of companies incorporated in the United Kingdom at the time of issue (such issues are now very rare).

Formerly stamp duty was payable, once for all, on foreign bearer bonds and share certificates in "American form" but this was rescinded by the Finance Act of 1967.

STOCK. This term includes both stocks and shares.

STOCK EXCHANGE OFFICIAL LIST. A list of all quoted securities except a few inactive stocks which appear in the Monthly Supplementary List. The S.E.O.L. gives particulars of the latest dividend, date x.d. and date of payment, the official quotation at 2.15 p.m., and prices at which bargains have been marked by that time. As the List is published at about 5.30 p.m. on each business day, changes in quotations made after 2.15 p.m. cannot be included. Market prices are usually much closer than the official quotations which are deliberately made rather wide to avoid incessant changes, and the prices in the morning newspapers are those ruling at the close of business; if news affecting the company concerned has appeared during the afternoon these may be quite different from the official quotations.

STOCK SPLIT. American term for capitalization issue. A three-for-two stock split is equivalent to a one-for-two capitalization issue. *See* page 82.

SUBSCRIPTION WARRANT. When Canadian companies raise fresh money by means of a rights issue, instead of sending out Provisional Allotment letters, they issue Subscription Warrants entitling the holder to take up new shares at the issue price. *See* page 77.

SWITCH. The substitution of one investment for another. In the "gilt edged" market large switches are commonplace, and the jobber may well deal inside his price in one of the transactions.

TAKE IN. One who has sold stock which he either does not possess or does not wish to deliver, is said to "take in" the stock which he borrows from a bull to deliver against his sale. *See* article on CONTANGOS.

TALON. Share warrants to bearer have a sheet of numbered coupons attached. One of these is cut off each time that the company declares a dividend and surrendered against payment of the dividend. The last coupon is called the "talon" (French for heel), and this is surrendered against a new sheet of coupons.

TAP LOANS. British Government loans have usually been floated by announcing that the Government wished to borrow so many million pounds and inviting subscriptions by prospectus stating the price of issue, rate of interest and redemption dates (or a statement that the loan was to be irredeemable); the lists were closed when the full amount had been subscribed or if the full amount was not obtained, after a few days, when the outstanding balance would be taken by Government Departments and sold in the market as opportunity offered.

After the war it became the practice to issue loans, e.g. National War Bonds $2\frac{1}{2}\%$, to an unlimited amount, as required; these are described as being "on tap" or "tap loans"; when sufficient money has been obtained or when the currency of the loan is getting too short, the tap is turned off and a new loan on similar terms but with different (slightly later) redemption dates is put "on tap" in its place.

TAX VOUCHER. Dividend warrants sent to registered shareholders are accompanied by a voucher showing the number of shares and the net amount paid and stating that tax has been deducted and will be paid or accounted for to the proper authority. Some vouchers show the gross amount of the dividend and the tax deducted but most leave the recipient to work out the gross amount from the tables printed on the back of the voucher.

In the case of shares in bearer or in American form the bank collects the dividend and issues a tax voucher; in this case the voucher has to be signed by the shareholder before being sent to H.M. Inspector of Taxes in support of a claim.

TOUCH. This is a very close price usually only to be found in an active and free market. *See* page 14.

TRANSFER. Abbreviation for DEED OF TRANSFER.

UNDER. Under means $\frac{1}{32}$ of £1 or $3\frac{1}{8}$p. Thus a price quoted "under to three-quarters," means $\frac{1}{32}$ under $\frac{3}{4}$ (or $\frac{23}{32}$) to $\frac{3}{4}$ or £0·71$\frac{7}{8}$ to£ 0·75; there may or may not be a big figure. "Under" must be carefully distinguished from "and under" which means $\frac{1}{64}$ under the price. Thus "eleven-sixteenths to three-quarters and under" means $\frac{11}{16}$ to $\frac{47}{64}$ (or $\frac{23}{32} + \frac{1}{64}$ as it is usually written) or £0·68$\frac{3}{4}$ to £0·73$\frac{7}{16}$.

UNSECURED LOAN. A number of companies of impeccable financial standing have raised money by the issue of unsecured loans, their credit being so good that they have not found it necessary to issue debentures secured on the general assets or on specific properties and with a trustee to protect the interests of those lending the money.

VENDOR SHARES. Shares in company "A" issued to the seller, instead of cash, in payment for shares in company "B" or any other assets being acquired by company "A".

VOUCHER, CAPITAL GAINS. *See* chapter on capital gains tax.

VOUCHER, TAX. *See* TAX VOUCHER.

WARRANT, DIVIDEND. Cheques sent out in payment of dividends are called dividend warrants.

WARRANT. Stock or share warrant to bearer. Bearer stock or bearer shares.

WARRANT. Some companies have issued loan stocks with detachable "warrants to subscribe" for ordinary shares. These warrants may either be surrendered with the loan stock on specified dates for its conversion into ordinary shares or, may be used, with cash, to subscribe for ordinary shares at a given price. In the meantime both loan stock and warrants are quoted separately, and the latter may be regarded as long term option money.

X.D. Abbreviation for ex dividend.

X.R. Abbreviation for ex rights. More often "x.rts."

YIELD. The annual return on the money invested in the security in question at the current price.

Nicknames of Stocks and Shares

MANY stocks and shares are often referred to by abbreviated titles or by nicknames; in the majority of cases it is obvious which stock is meant, though the origin of a few of the names is obscure. The investor wishing to look up particulars of a stock should, if he is at first unable to find it, look under the following prefixes: Amalgamated, Anglo-, Associated, British, Imperial, International, National, New, Royal, United, etc. For "Rhodesian" he should now look under "Zambian". Surnames sometimes appear to be Christian names particularly if a letter has been dropped out, e.g. there is at present no William Hudson to be found under "H" but there is a Williams Hudson to be found under "W".

In response to numerous requests a list is given of some of the more generally used nicknames, together with the securities to which they refer.

AMERICAN CELANESE: Celanese Corporation of America.
ANZAC BANK: Australia and New Zealand Banking Group
BATS: British American Tobacco.
BAYS: Hudson's Bay Company.
B.I.C.C.: British Insulated Callender's Cables
B.P.C.: British Printing Corporation
BRICKS: London Brick Company.
B.S.A.: Birmingham Small Arms.
CANPACS: Canadian Pacific Railway.
CANTABS: Imperial Tobacco Company of Canada.
CASTS: Consolidated African Selection Trust.
CEMENT: Associated Portland Cement.
CHEMICALS: Imperial Chemical Industries.
COAL 3½%: Treasury 3½% stock 1977/80.
CRITS: Consolidated Rand Investment Trust.
DALTONS: Treasury 2½% 1975 or after.
D.R.G.: Dickinson Robinson Group
DUTCH: Royal Dutch Petroleum.
EDITH: Estate Duties Investment Trust.
E.M.I.s or EMMIES: Electric & Musical Industries.
FREDDIES: Free State Development and Investment Corporation (Orange Free State).
GEOFFRIES: General Exploration Orange Free State.

GUSSIES: Great Universal Stores.

HARTIES: Hartebeestfontein Gold Mining

HAY'S WHARF: Proprietors of Hay's Wharf. It appears under "P" in the Official List and under "H" in some newspapers.

I.C.G.: Imperial Continental Gas.

I.C. HOLDINGS: International Computer Holdings.

IKEYS or I.C.I.s: Imperial Chemical Industries.

I.M.I.: Imperial Metal Industries

IMPS: Imperial Tobacco Company (of Great Britain and Ireland).

JOHNNIES: Johannesburg Consolidated Investment Company.

MAMS: Management Agency and Music

NICKELS: International Nickel of Canada.

OFSITS: Orange Free State Investment Trust.

POTS PLATS: Potgietersrust Platinum

SAINTS: Scottish American Investment Trust

SALLIES: South African Lands.

SIDRO: Société Internationale d'Energie Hydro-Electrique Sidro.

SLUBBERS: British Cotton and Wool Dyers' Association.

SOFINA: Société Financière. de Transport et d'Entreprises Industrielles.

STEEL: $3\frac{1}{2}$%: Treasury $3\frac{1}{2}$% 1979/81.

SUITS: Scottish and Universal Investment Trust.

SWINES: South African Distilleries and Wines.

TACE: Transport and Chemical Engineering.

TANKS: Tanganyika Concessions.

TRACKIES: Brascan (formerly Brazilian Power, Light and Traction).

WAGONS: British Transport 3% 1968/73.

WOOLLIES: Woolworth.

WRITS: West Rand Investment Trust.

Z.C.I. Zambia Copper Investments.

Index

Talon, 204
Tap loans, 204
Tax, Double Relief, 106 *seq.*
Tender, 69
Ticket, 30, 49, 157, 165
Trace, 158
Transfer, 21, 30 *seq.*
Trustee securities, 83 *seq.*

UNDER, 205
Unit trusts, 126 *seq.*
Unsecured loan, 205

VALUATION—
   for Probate, 60
   of assets, 62 *seq.*
   of rights, 78
Value—
   break-up, 63
   nominal, 9, 39
   no par, 9, 90

Vendor shares, 180
Voucher—
   capitalg ains, 128
   tax, 204

WARRANT—
   dividend, 205
   subscription, 77
   to bearer, 205
Wasting assets, 61
Wider range, 83 *seq.*

X CAPITALIZATION, 73, 198
      see also Ex capitalization.
x.d. 41 *seq.*, 159 *seq.*, 161, 205
x.rts, (ex rights), 78, 205

YIELD, 89 *seq.*, 205
   with redemption, 92 *seq.*, 98